The Temple
of Edfu

The Temple *of* Edfu

A Guide by
an Ancient Egyptian Priest

Dieter Kurth

Translated by Anthony Alcock

The American University in Cairo Press

Cairo — New York

English translation copyright © 2004 by
The American University in Cairo Press
113 Sharia Kasr el Aini, Cairo, Egypt
420 Fifth Avenue, New York, NY 10018
www.aucpress.com

First published in German in 1994 as *Edfu: Ein ägyptischer Tempel gesehen mit den Augen der alten Ägypter.*
Copyright © 1994 by Wissenschaftliche Buchgesellschaft, Darmstadt.
Protected under the Berne Convention

Dar el Kutub No. 11672/02
ISBN 978 977 424 764 4

3 4 5 6 7 8 9 10 11 12   12 11 10 09 08 07

Designed by Andrea El-Akshar/AUC Press Design Center
Printed in Egypt

Contents

Illustrations

Preface

The central part of this little book contains a translation of the hieroglyphic text copied from the enclosure wall of the temple of Edfu (fig. 1). It has been a long journey from the first copies made in the nineteenth century—in successive stages, each stage preparing the way for the next one—to the translation presented here. The Egyptologists Heinrich Karl Brugsch and Johannes Dümichen copied the text in the nineteenth century, which was a pioneer achievement; the many errors were due largely to the difficult working conditions of the time. The copy of the hieroglyphic text that has now become standard and is considered reliable was made in 1932 by Émile Chassinat (fig. 2). The first reliable translation was made in 1961 by Constant de Wit.

The Edfu Project, which I initiated in 1986, was very generously supported by the German Research Council (DFG) and thereafter taken over into the program of the Göttingen Academy of Humanities and Sciences. This support has enabled us to continue the long-term work involved in achieving a secure epigraphic basis for the temple inscriptions and carrying out systematic philological work on the corpus of Edfu texts, which have both had a beneficial effect on the translation of the text that forms the core of this small volume.

Fig. 1: Northwest corner and west side of the enclosure wall. To the left, under the feet of the two figures, one can see a section of the long band of inscription containing the text.

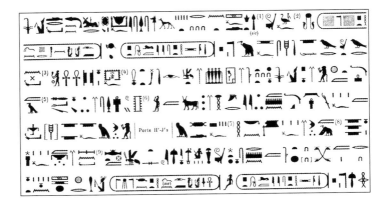

Fig. 2: A page from the publication of Émile Chassinat, *Le Temple
d'Edfou*. It corresponds to the text on both sides of the northern
door in the west side of the enclosure wall (H'J'2 and fig. 1).

I would like to warmly thank Andreas Effland and Jan-
Peter Graeff for their valuable help in choosing, designing,
and preparing the illustrations, the former also for establishing
the bibliography.

A few notes on the text:

1. The Glossary contains information about special terms and
the various deities.

2. The description of the temple in the translation follows the
ground plan that is printed on the inside cover (front and back)
of the book and is thus easy to consult. The capital letters in the
ground plan appear in the appropriate passages of the translation
referring to topographical details. Figures 32–38 show some of
the reliefs mentioned in the relevant passages of the translation.
These reliefs can easily be found in the temple itself by those for-
tunate enough to visit the site, with the help of the capital letters
on the ground plan. But even without the illustrations, it is possible to locate other reliefs in the temple just by using the details in
the translation, since many of them are immediately recognizable.

3. The terms 'left' and 'right' refer to the perspective of some-one standing in the temple and looking toward the entrance.

4. Text in brackets has been restored by the author, e.g., [king of] Egypt. Text in parentheses gives additional information, e.g., the greatest god (Horus). Ellipses within brackets—[. . .]—indicate lost hieroglyphs that cannot be restored. Ellipses not enclosed in brackets or parentheses—. . .—indicate text intentionally left out by the author. Royal names in cartouches on the wall inscription are represented in the text in bold typeface.

5. Dates for the Old, Middle, and New kingdoms follow *The British Museum Dictionary of Ancient Egypt* by Ian Shaw and Paul Nicholson.

Fig. 3 (following page): View of the corridor of the temple.

Introduction

The town of Edfu is in Upper Egypt (fig. 4), about halfway between Luxor and Aswan. It is the site of the temple of the god Horus, the best preserved temple of the ancient world. Horus was worshipped there in the company of his beautiful consort Hathor of Dendera and their son Harsomtus (fig. 5). This book concentrates upon the main temple of Edfu, but we should bear in mind that there are other temples and shrines situated round the huge temple of Horus, including, for instance, the birth-house (Mammisi) of the divine child Harsomtus. Moreover, a great part of the holy precinct has yet to be excavated, as well as the ancient town, the ruins of which tower to the west of the Horus Temple.

The temple of Horus is covered with thousands of inscriptions (fig. 3 and cover). They can be seen everywhere: on walls, columns, ceilings, and even on dadoes, flagpole niches, and the bases of the lion waterspouts.

One of the inscriptions contains the text translated in this book. This ancient text makes an excellent guidebook, for its author was one of the finest experts on the temple. Who was he? He was an Egyptian who lived in Edfu about 2,100 years ago and was one of the high-ranking priests responsible for design-

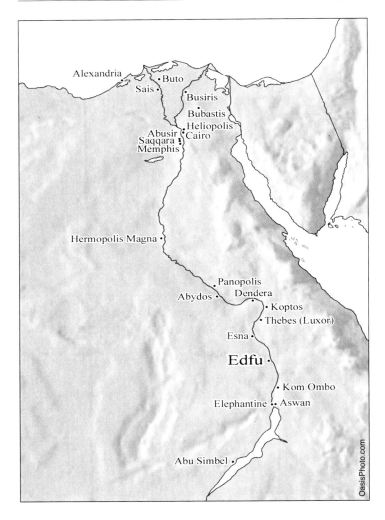

Fig. 4: Map of Egypt.

ing the texts that would decorate the temple. Although more than a hundred years had elapsed since construction of the temple had begun in 237 B.C., he was intimately acquainted with the building history of the temple in all its phases.

His information came from papyrus records and the priestly tradition, since he was one of the scholars of Edfu. Whether he lived to see the completion of the building in 57 B.C. we do not know. We do not even know his name.

The text, which I have simply translated here, was not of course written as a guidebook. Its purpose was to create an inscription that would be suitable for the place where it was to be carved: on the outer surface of the enclosure wall (J'), where it was to run for some 300 meters in a horizontal inscription band around the lower part of the entire wall (fig. 1).

It is usually the case that the lower horizontal inscription band of any temple refers to the building history, layout, or functions of its individual parts. The text was thus fixed and became an excellent guidebook: as the temple itself was completely surrounded by the great enclosure wall, the complete building work was described in the inscription band, with its history, architectural composition, individual rooms, even down to the staircases, doors, and locks.

The description is planned, accurate, detailed, and complete. If we allow ourselves to be guided through the temple by the author of this inscription, we shall see the building with the eyes of a competent contemporary, a priest of Edfu who composed this text about 100 B.C.

An observation on the content of the text may be made here. Some passages, with their effusive praise of the temple, may strike modern visitors looking at the grey temple walls as somewhat exaggerated. It should he borne in mind, however, that the whole of the temple was once brightly colored. In some places there are still traces of the original color: for example, the underside of the lintel over the main entrance of the Outer Hypostyle Hall (C') as well as the ceiling and the column capital in the northwest corner of this hall.

Fig. 5: The king makes an offering to Horus, Hathor, and Harsomtus
the Child, the lords of the Edfu Temple.

Edfu is not the only Egyptian temple for which ancient statements concerning deities, functions, builders, and general appearance have been preserved. The earliest building inscriptions date back to the Old Kingdom (c.2686–2181 B.C.); there are also inscriptions, especially from the New Kingdom (c.1550–1069 B.C.), made by visitors who wished to record their impressions of a temple that was already for them an ancient building.

Some of these inscriptions will be quoted in the following brief excursion through the long history of Egyptian temple-building.

Temples and Believers
in Ancient Egypt

The most common Egyptian name for a temple is *het-netjer* (pronounced in the later period something like *heneete*), which literally means 'mansion of the god.' It was where the god lived on earth. He took up residence in the statues of his temple and made these statues part of himself.

The whole nature of the god was inscrutable—it could not be comprehended or depicted. But human beings were able to know and imitate some of the deity's forms. Thus, the god Ra revealed himself mainly in his sun-disk, but also in the form of a lion, a cat, or an ichneumon. In each of these forms the god acted in a particular way.

All natural events were understood as actions of the gods. The waning and waxing of the moon, the receding and swelling waters of the Nile flood, and the 'burial' and 'revival' of grain were attributed to the actions of Osiris: everything that periodically had to die was revived by his power. The sky-goddess Nut was responsible for the daily rising and setting of the sun, the moon, and the stars. In the course of every day she swallowed the heavenly bodies and caused them to be reborn. Nut had the form of a woman bending over or a cow whose body forms the vault of heaven, in which the heavenly bodies move.

Because their actions were revealed in all things, the gods had an inexhaustible supply of manifestations. The forms depicted in statues and reliefs represent only some of these: pure animal form, mixed animal form, human form, and mixed animal-human form (fig. 5). The mixed forms made it possible to combine several natural characteristics and to express more complex divine action.

The statues were made from precious materials, both stone and metal, especially gold, since gold was considered to be the flesh of the gods. One of the statues stood in the sanctuary as the main cult image of the god. Every morning this image was purified with incense, washed, clothed, and anointed. The god present in the statue was provided with offerings by the priests, who also sang hymns of praise to the god.

This sort of treatment shows that the cult image was regarded as a living being, in which the god was present and could be addressed by human beings. But the god took up residence in the cult image, as it were to bring it to life, only under certain conditions—the statue had to be suitable and in a temple that corresponded to the god's nature.

Because the nature of the god had a cosmic dimension, the temple, in its layout and decoration, was modeled on the world. The dadoes of its walls were decorated with plants and animals, representing the earth, the ceilings of its rooms were lavishly decorated with stars representing heaven, and the supporting columns were meant to represent plants and trees (figs. 6 and 20).

Every Egyptian temple had this appearance: it was a copy of the world. In inscriptions of the Greco-Roman period the temple was even named 'heaven' or 'horizon.' The large temple complex of Karnak was known as 'Heaven on Earth.'

The temple had to be pure if the god was to accept it as his house. Purity began with the building itself: no noise or impurity was allowed inside the temple. This is why the temple was carefully swept, sprayed with water, and purified with incense to remove even those impurities that might hover in the air.

Fig. 6: Reconstructed view of Philae Temple from the *Description de l'Égypte*.

The priests too had to be pure when they performed their duties. Purification consisted partly in washing thoroughly, chewing natron, shaving the hair, and donning white garments. But external purity alone was not enough, and priests were also obliged to demonstrate pure behavior, including the avoidance of impure food and at least temporary sexual abstinence.

Ideally, the Egyptian king himself was the high priest in all temples, but in practice he was represented in the daily cult by the so-called Royal Priest. The numerous ritual scenes depicted in the temples still show us details of the contents and performance of offerings made by the king to the god (fig. 32ff.): he brought the god food and drink, flowers, clothing, jewelry, and amulets; he played the sistrum for the god; he danced; he performed the ritual running; he killed the enemies of the god.

In return the god gave him everything that would maintain the king, Egypt, and the world, including health, long life, plentiful harvests, victory over the enemies of Egypt, the submission of other countries, and the continuance of heaven and the heavenly bodies. This latter gift referred especially to the sun, for it was known that the light of the sun was the precondition of life.

Thus the offerings of the king were an indispensable necessity, for his daily service in the temple guaranteed the stability of the state and maintenance of the world. To express this cosmic dimension of the temple-cult, the temple itself was designed in the form of a cosmic building. In this respect the temple is fundamentally different from a Christian church, which is nowadays principally a place where the individual worshipper through prayer seeks a personal relationship with God.

The Egyptian temple allowed only limited scope for expression of personal piety. The general public was not permitted access to the interior of the temple. Only on certain occasions were ordinary people allowed to enter the great forecourt of the temple (H' in the plan), and among other things the forecourt was known as the Court of the Multitude. In addition, people could use a small cult area in the outer wall of some temples in order to tell the god of their personal concerns and ask for help. The god of this area in the temple of Kom Ombo is described as "The Lord of the Two Wedjat Eyes, with numerous ears, who hears the request of everyone."

A larger number of believers were able to come into contact with their god when the portable cult image was taken outside the temple on festival days. Bareheaded priests would carry it on their shoulders out of the semi-darkness of the temple. Large numbers of people would line the processional way. They worshipped the passing cult image and prostrated themselves on the ground before it, or they waited for the answer that the god would give to their personal petitions—the statue would tilt either toward or away from the petitioner.

Hundreds of temples were built in the Nile Valley, and some were constructed even in the remote oases of the Libyan Desert

and the valleys of the Eastern Desert. They all followed more or
less the same plan in their cosmic architecture and basic decora-
tive schemes and in the relationship between god and temple.
There were, however, considerable differences in details. In addition to the constructed temples, there were also temples, such as
that at Abu Simbel, which were hewn out of the rock, what one
might call 'negative architecture.' Some temples have a single
symmetrical axis, others go off at an angle. Some temples have
only one sanctuary, others have two or more, with the appropriate extensions. On the other hand, there are temples, principally
those devoted to the cult of the sun-god, with altars situated in
large open courts.

This variety of forms is due partly to the purposes for which
the temple was intended and partly to changes in the religion over
time. Another reason is that from the very beginning individual
theological systems had emerged in different temples. These
systems developed further by inspiring each other at certain
points, which in turn created fertile soil for the highly imaginative
and very sophisticated theological thought that we encounter in
the texts of many temples. Religious pluralism and relative toler-
ance were marked features of ancient Egyptian religious life.
This picture was not greatly disturbed by the religious revolution
of Akhenaten, a period of religious intolerance and dogmatism
that lasted only about two decades.

The many deities worshiped in Egyptian temples possessed
qualities that were both common and individual. Gods renowned
for one of their qualities in all Egypt and who could deputize for
many were the ram-headed creator Khnum of Elephantine, the
falcon-headed warrior Horus of Edfu, the primeval and creator-
god Amun of Thebes, the goddess of music, ecstasy, and love,
Hathor of Dendera, the omniscient ibis-headed god Thoth of
Hermopolis, the sun and creator-god Ra of Heliopolis, the cat-
headed goddess of fertility Bastet of Bubastis, and the snake-
shaped tutelary goddess of Lower Egypt, Uto of Buto.

What they all had in common was divine nature, and in their

temples each of them was the omnipresent creator of all that exists. That is why there could be temples with more than one principal god and why gods could be received as guest deities in temples not their own. This also made possible the formation of divine families, which often consisted of father, mother, and son (triads). Mutual recognition also led to a closer association between certain gods, who even traveled long distances to visit each other.

The layout of the temple was also influenced by these various relationships. This can be seen in temples with several sanctuaries, chapels for guest divinities, even in the processional ways lined by sphinxes and the position of certain gates. The conclusion may be drawn that temple building and religion in ancient Egypt shared a universally valid framework in which there were many individual variations, and which itself did not remain unchanged but was constantly expanded by developments within the religion.

Because of the long and complex history of Egyptian religion this brief survey of the relationship among temple, god, and believer has had to be limited to a particular historical period, from the New Kingdom to the end of Egyptian religious history in the early centuries of Christianity, but the following survey of the temple buildings themselves begins with the earliest known period.

Figure 7 shows an ivory tablet from the time of King Aha of the First Dynasty (c.3000 B.C.). The cult emblem of the goddess Neith with two crossed arrows stands in an open courtyard. To the left, at the entrance of the courtyard, are two masts, perhaps the predecessors of the later flagpoles that were erected in niches of the façade of the pylons. If so, the triangles at the top of each pole would represent a strip of cloth. The building itself stands in the rear part of the courtyard.

Figure 8 shows a seal-impression dating from the time of King Djer of the First Dynasty. The form of the shrine is unexpected: the building was apparently modeled, partly or wholly, on an animal, but the kind of the animal cannot be determined with certainty. The building materials for architecture of this sort could only have been wood and matting.

Fig. 7: Ivory tablet from the time of King Aha with a representation of the sanctuary of the goddess Neith, above, and a reconstruction of what it may have looked like, below.

Fig. 8: Seal-impressions from the time of King Djer with
a representation of an animal-shaped sanctuary.

Figure 10 shows the first monumental building in stone: the
Step Pyramid of King Djoser of the Third Dynasty (c.2600 B.C.).
The pyramid and its precinct are in Saqqara belonging to the
'West of Memphis,' which was a common designation for the
cemeteries of the capital, Memphis. Whereas the pyramid itself is
now denuded of its original limestone casing and thus has a
coarse and rough appearance, the buildings in the foreground still
have their casing. Many of the buildings in the Djoser precinct
are 'dummy' buildings: the finely polished and close fitting Tura
limestone conceals massive building elements and imitates wood-
en beams, bundles of reeds, and half-opened doors.

The whole pyramid precinct was much bigger than figure 10
indicates. It also contains several courtyards, a large altar, and
other buildings, including a mortuary temple (fig. 9). Its existence

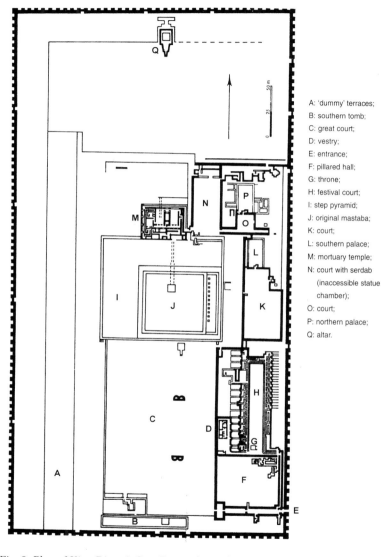

A: 'dummy' terraces;
B: southern tomb;
C: great court;
D: vestry;
E: entrance;
F: pillared hall;
G: throne;
H: festival court;
I: step pyramid;
J: original mastaba;
K: court;
L: southern palace;
M: mortuary temple;
N: court with serdab
   (inaccessible statue
   chamber);
O: court;
P: northern palace;
Q: altar.

Fig. 9: Plan of King Djoser's Step Pyramid complex at Saqqara.

Fig. 10: The pyramid of King Djoser at Saqqara.

proves that temples were erected not only for gods, but also for the dead king. It was in these mortuary temples that the dead kings were able to live on in their statues, receiving offerings and worship from their priests, just like the gods.

A divine nature was attributed to the king, especially in the Old Kingdom. As the living king, he stood between god and man and had divine and human qualities. He was mortal, but it could be said of him: "You are the god Ra in the body, his body is your body." But the dead king became totally divine. In the Pyramid Texts the sky-goddess Nut says to him: "You shall open up your place in heaven among the stars of heaven." In another passage it is said of the dead king: "He is a god, who is older than the oldest. He is served by thousands and receives offerings from hundreds."

The Fourth Dynasty sees the emergence of the classical form of the pyramid. The pyramid complex now embraces a mortuary temple on the east side of the pyramid and a covered way leading from the mortuary temple to the valley temple. Figure 12, which shows a pyramid complex of the Fifth Dynasty, displays the individual building elements. The valley temple was most probably used only for the burial rites and then sealed. Figure 11 shows a reconstruction of the inside of the valley temple belonging to the pyramid complex of King Khafra. The heavy pillars were of pink granite, the floor of alabaster; narrow openings high up in the wall allowed light to shine on the green diorite statues of the king. The combination of architecture, building material, and lighting system was harmonious, and in my opinion also designed to achieve an aesthetic effect, in addition to the religious symbolism of the colors and light.

It is clear from figure 12, showing the pyramid complex of the Fifth Dynasty King Sahura, that the mortuary temple was attached to the pyramid, which meant that the tomb and the cult area were directly connected. Later, in the New Kingdom, the royal tomb and the mortuary temple were to be separated from each other: the tomb was laid out underground in the remote Valley of the Kings to protect it from the highly successful ancient Egyptian tomb robbers, the mortuary temple being some distance away on the edge of the cultivated land. The royal mortuary temple of the New Kingdom was only partly devoted to the cult of the king. It was principally a temple to the gods. In this way the cult of the dead ruler came under the protection of the god, and he would receive his offerings as long as the temple continued to function.

Egyptians of the New Kingdom were frequent visitors to the (by then) thousand-year-old pyramid complexes and left graffiti in the pyramids, the mortuary temples, and subsidiary buildings. The scribe Ahmose, in the course of a visit to the mortuary temple of Djoser, felt that it "was as if the sky were in it and the sun were rising." He made a wish: "May there be offerings of bread, cattle, fowl, and all good and pure things to the Ka of the blessed King Djoser. May heaven cause fresh myrrh to fall as rain and incense to fall as drops." The scribe Kha-em-men-nefer came to the same place to see the wonder.

Fig. 11: Valley temple of King Khafra: reconstruction
showing statues of the king.

The following inscription, also from the temple precinct of Djoser in Saqqara, records the reason for the visit:

"Regnal year 47, 2nd month of the season of Peret, day 25. The scribe of the treasury, Hadnakhte, son of Sewel and Tauseret, came for a pleasant stroll in the West of Memphis with his brother Panakhte, the scribe of the vizier. Words to be spoken: 'All you gods of the West of Memphis, divine Ennead and First of the realm of the dead, Osiris, Isis, and you great and blessed dead of the West of Ankhtawi (Memphis), grant me a beautiful long life in the service of your Kas and later a fine burial after a good old age, so that I can see for myself the West of Memphis as a member of that blessed community, like you.' Written by the scribe of the treasury of the Lord of the Two Lands (the king), Hadnakhte, blessed, together with the scribe Panakhte."

One visitor complains of the inscriptions made by his predecessors:

"The scribe with the clever fingers, the clever scribe without equal in Memphis, Amen-em-het. I say: 'Explain these words to me. My heart is sick when I see the work of their hands . . . . It is like the work of a stupid woman. Somebody should have accused them before they were allowed to visit the temple. Their work is awful. They are not scribes trained by Thoth (god of writing).'" This sort of vanity and verbal abuse of the colleagues' professional ability may seem ill-judged to us, but it does indeed show a certain consciousness of quality.

A graffito on the wall of the mortuary temple of King Sahura in Abusir says: "Second regnal year, 3rd month of the season of Akhet, day 7, under the Majesty of the King of Upper and Lower Eygpt [. . .] life, health and prosperity. The scribe Amen-em-het . . . came to visit the temple of his Majesty, the King of Upper and Lower Egypt Sahura, blessed. He found it pleasing to his heart. It seemed to him like the moonlit sky. Thereupon he said: 'How beautiful is the [temple for the Ka] of His Majesty, the King of Upper and Lower Egypt Sahura, blessed. [. . .] Cattle, fowl, and bread [. . .].'"

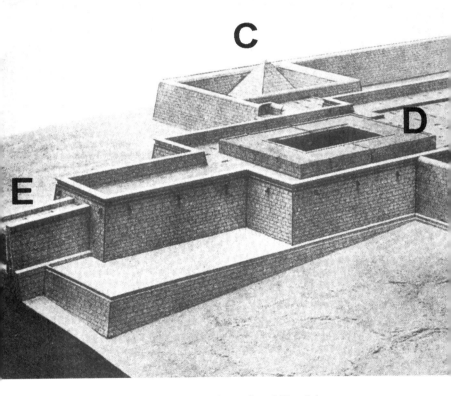

Fig. 12: Pyramid complex of King Sahura
at Abusir: reconstruction.

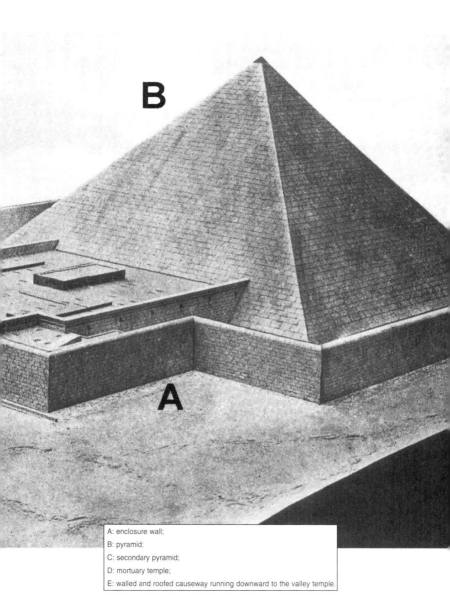

A: enclosure wall;
B: pyramid;
C: secondary pyramid;
D: mortuary temple;
E: walled and roofed causeway running downward to the valley temple.

The text, written in the reign of Amenhotep II or Thutmose IV in black ink, is about one thousand years younger than the temple itself. It ends, as far one can tell from its rather fragmentary condition, with a request for offerings. It was composed in the hieratic script (fig. 14), the cursive or scribal form of hieroglyphs. Hieratic was the everyday script and written mostly on

Fig. 13: A ritual scene from the temple of King Sety I at Abydos.

papyrus, whereas hieroglyphs were a sort of monumental script used principally to decorate tombs and temples (figs. 2, 5, and 13). In both scripts all signs are pictures, which within the writing system carry partly phonetic and partly pictorial values. In the hieratic script the pictures are much abbreviated and cannot be recognized instantly but have to be learned.

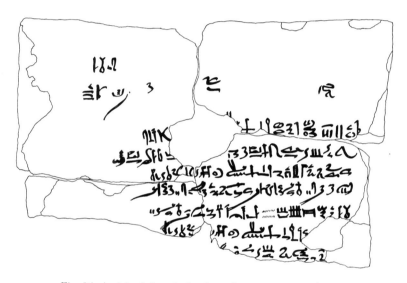

Fig. 14: A visitor's inscription from the mortuary temple of King Sahura at Abusir.

What were the reasons for these visits? To some extent, it was a form of ancient 'tourism'; people went to visit the impressive monuments of former kings for pleasure. By the New Kingdom, in most cases, a cult was no longer performed in these monuments, and they were more or less generally accessible. Naturally, visitors were also aware of the holiness of the place, as is shown by the prayers and requests for offerings, and they were hopeful that here too they would gain something for their own afterlife.

Fig. 15: Processional chapel of King Senusret I at Karnak
(reconstructed in the Open Air Museum).

There is not much left to see of Middle Kingdom
(c.2055–1650 B.C.) temples, apart from a small chapel of King
Senusret I, used to set down the processional bark while offerings
were being made (fig. 15). But even this small shrine had to be
reconstructed from its dismantled stones, which had been reused
in antiquity as filling material for a later building. The reconstruction by Egyptologists was worth the effort: its reliefs are
among the finest ever made by ancient Egyptians.

Several large temples have survived from the New Kingdom
(c.1500–1069 B.C.), but they too have had to be partially reconstructed. However, the temples of Abydos, Medinet Habu,
Luxor, and Karnak, to name only a few of the most famous, were
so well preserved that even before their reconstruction they were
able to impress modern travelers. This is evident from the many
graffiti left on the walls of these temples by European visitors of
the last two or three centuries, perhaps in an attempt to achieve a
bit of immortality. Today, the temples have been reconstructed

Fig. 16: View of the Great Hypostyle Hall of the temple
of Karnak with clerestory windows.

and millions of tourists visit Egypt. The effect of the great
pharaonic buildings is now greater, as indeed is the temptation to
leave a 'calling card' for posterity, but this is now prohibited.

Figure 16 shows a view of the inside of the Great Hypostyle
Hall at Karnak (thirteenth century B.C.), where one can see two
north–south rows of columns (of the 134 located in the hall) and
a clerestory window with its stone lattice intact. One gets an idea
of the enormous size of these columns from the man standing
near the left-hand row: the twelve columns of the middle row are
22.40 meters high (including their abacus), the others (minus
abacus) are a 'mere' 14.74 meters. The two lower column rows,
left and right of the twelve middle columns, were built up to their
height and fitted with lattice windows; these four rows between
them bear the weight of the roof of the three raised middle aisles,
through whose side windows light penetrated into the temple.

Figure 13 shows an almost completely intact relief, with all its
colors. It comes from the temple of King Sety I at Abydos (beginning of the thirteenth century B.C.). The artistry and craftsman-
ship of the reliefs made in the time of Sety I are almost without
equal. The scene shows, to the left, Sety I transfigured into a god.
Holding a flagellum and a regal staff, the insignia of the murdered
and resurrected god Osiris, in which form Sety himself has come
back to life. Before the king stands the god Iunmutef, making an
offering. Iunmutef makes the purifying strength of his offering
effective by pronouncing the spell recorded above and behind
him in hieroglyphs. Iunmutef wears the side-lock of youth and
panther-skin that characterize him as the eldest son and successor of the king, whose duty it was to perform the funerary offerings for his dead father.

New Kingdom temples often contain building inscriptions
mentioning the king responsible for the temple and the god to
whom it was dedicated. Occasionally, the inscriptions contain an
assessment of the work. The following text comes from Karnak:
"May . . . the King of Upper and Lower Egypt, Lord of the Two
Lands (Rameses IX) live. He built it as a monument for his father

Amun-Ra, king of the gods, creating a large gate from beautiful clear sandstone . . . ."

Another text in the same temple: "He (Ramesses II) made it as his monument for his father Amun-Ra, Lord of the Thrones of the Two Lands, rebuilding the temple for him from beautiful clear sandstone, a magnificent work for eternity. Its wall reaches up to heaven . . . . It was the god Ptah who issued instructions (for the building), while Thoth put them into writing. The tightening and loosening of the measuring rope (were performed) by the King himself and the goddess Seshat. It was built from stone as a work for eternity, in order to make his (the god's) house splendid, lasting until the end of time."

There are also building inscriptions in temples constructed before and after the New Kingdom down to the time of Roman rule in Egypt. But these texts rarely contain precise information, for example, about the building history, or the dimensions of the temple or the appointment of its rooms. For the most part they mention only the founder of the temple and the god, contenting themselves with brief and very general information about the nature of the building. More detailed descriptions of temple buildings occur only in the Greco-Roman period, in the temples of Dendera and Edfu.

The building inscription of Edfu, however, is unique. It certainly contains information and formulae that occur in other building inscriptions, but the extent, precision, and detail of the Edfu text are unparalleled.

The impressive temple site towers above the houses of modern Efdu (fig. 17). But even though the modern houses crowd around the temple, you enter another world as you pass through the pylon, the double towered gate. The ten-meter high enclosure wall of the temple keeps the earthly house of the god apart from the outside world.

The great open courtyard induces a feeling of peace and harmony, with its architecture and decoration that combine many different forms and signs according to strict rules. After leaving

Fig. 17: Aerial view of the temple of Edfu.

the open courtyard, you enter a columned hall (see cover) and proceed through doors and rooms that decrease in width and height, thus being guided in a straight line, until you reach the sanctuary, the most intimate part of the temple, where the god was always present in his cult image.

The best way to get an idea of the effect that the temple had on the priests and believers of that time, and what it meant to them, is to read the great and unique building inscription of the temple of Edfu.

The Discovery
of the Edfu Temple

Before it became possible to read and study the great building inscription of Edfu, the temple had to be discovered, cleared of the accumulated rubbish of the previous 1,500 years, and scientifically surveyed and recorded.

We do not know when the cult of Horus came to an end, when the last priest entered the sanctuary for the last time in order to perform the ancient rites before his god and bring him offerings. It may have been at the beginning of the fifth century A.D., not long after the Emperor Theodosius I had forbidden other religions and made Christianity the exclusive religion of his empire. But it may also have happened decades before or after this date since on the one hand, most of the population of Egypt had become Christian during the fourth century, and on the other hand, the cult of the goddess Isis on the island of Philae, only 100 kilometers to the south of Edfu, survived until the beginning of the sixth century.

Already in the middle of the fourth century, Christians were living near the town of Edfu, and there may have been a monastery there at the time. The adherents of the old religion may have been able to assert themselves alongside the Christians for a time, but their numbers gradually dwindled until only a few of the faithful gathered around the temple of Horus.

They were unable to keep up the full performance of the traditional cult because they were too few, their economic resources too small, and the temple too large. They probably ended up by worshipping their gods in only a few rooms, while other rooms were filled with rubbish or were being used as storage rooms or houses. This may have been how the cult of the temple slowly died out and came to an end, in a gradual process for which we have no firm historical evidence.

Finally, the Christian inhabitants of the town of Edfu took complete possession of the huge temple complex. They lived and worked in it, and they sought refuge behind its sturdy walls. Graffiti scratched into the stone or painted on the stone in red provide evidence of the life of the Christian inhabitants or of visitors to the temple. For example, on the roof of the temple there is a Coptic graffito: "Ankalomena, the son of the blessed Severus," followed by a Christian cross, and on the bridge between the pylon towers one can read Christian names like "Loukas" and "Maththaios." In another place we find

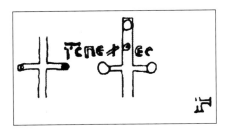

Fig. 18: Graffiti on the east wall
of the entrance corridor in
the western pylon tower.

large Coptic crosses and next to them the words "Jesus the Lord" (fig. 18). These Coptic graffiti have their pagan predecessors in Demotic: "The adoration of Padiharsomtus (son of) Panakht, son of Tu(tu) . . . (with following titles)" or "May the good name remain here permanently before Horus Behdety, the Great God, Lord of Heaven: Pakhi, (son of) Palehwe, (son of) Pakhôm" (fig. 19).

After the Arab Conquest (A.D. 640) the profane use of the temple continued. Mud brick huts began to crowd around the temple, occupying its roofs, and taking possession of its courtyards (fig. 20). Over the centuries a thin shroud of desert sand

Fig. 19: A Demotic graffito from the temple roof.

Fig. 21: The temple of Edfu, c.1800.

together with human settlement rubbish and refuse formed over the huge complex. Only the two pylon towers, the tops of the walls, and the roof area were still visible and testified to this mighty burial place of Egyptian belief (fig. 21).

Desert sand and settlement rubbish, on the other hand, also ensured that the temple of Edfu remained almost completely intact. They concealed the largest part of the reliefs and inscriptions and thus limited the amount of damage perpetrated by ignorant and superstitious descendants intent on hacking out the faces, arms, and legs of the images of the gods and kings (fig. 22).

Fig. 20: View from the pronaos to the large courtyard, c.1800.

Fig. 22: Faces, arms, and legs hacked out, on a scene from the inner face of the enclosure wall.

In around 630, Edfu became a bishopric and remained one for a few centuries after the Arab Conquest. The town is mentioned by Arab writers, and the well-known writer al-Maqrizi even reports on early archaeological activity: around A.D. 1300 a seated female figure with a Greek inscription was found.

Visitors' inscriptions provide us with information about the fate of the temple in the second millennium. Many visitors carved testimony of their presence into the masonry of the temple, while others in their detailed travel accounts describe the condition in which they found the temple.

Among the many Arabic graffiti from different periods, one in particular stands out (fig. 23). It is on the outside of the eastern enclosure wall, on the throne of the god Horus, in the third register, second ritual scene to the left, above the northern door. The scene, which the visitor can easily find if the light is good, depicts the king bringing an offering of incense to the gods Horus and Hathor. The brief Arabic text, which can be dated by the handwriting to the tenth or eleventh century, reads as follows:

"In the name of Allah the Merciful and Compassionate.

Think of me when I depart and say:

'May Allah bring you safely back home, stranger.'

We did think of you, stranger, and we said:

'May Allah bring you back home, safely and quite soon.'"

The stranger may have been passing through on the pilgrimage to Mecca. He was able to carve his text approximately seven meters above the current ground level, which means either that the accumulated rubbish was quite high or even perhaps that the roof of the inn where he was staying abutted onto the enclosure wall at this height.

In the account of his travels (1589), a Venetian visitor to the temple describes the Edfu pylon as the best preserved pylon he had seen and speaks of "a courtyard and a hypostyle hall with 50 columns." This is exactly the number of columns that can be counted in the courtyard and the pronaos (H' and C'). If he had gone farther into the temple (W), he would have been able to

Fig. 23: Arabic graffito on the outside of the eastern
enclosure wall, c.1000.

count 62 columns all together, but this was probably not possible at the time, because the inner area was filled to the ceiling with sand and rubbish.

The French travelers Claude Sicard and Nicholas Granger had a similar experience when they visited the temple between 1720 and 1731. Granger reports that the rubbish in the inner part of the temple reached almost to the ceiling and that the inhabitants of the mud brick huts on the roof would get rid of their garbage by throwing it through openings in the roof into the temple interior.

The French scholar François Jomard got as far as Edfu with Napoleon's army. His detailed account describes the sad condition of the main building:

"It was a matter of finding the place where the windows already mentioned had to be. This place . . . was on the right hand side of the roof, behind a small staircase . . . . Because the opening was blocked by a circle of mud bricks, I had to force my way in amid the cries and screams of the women and children. With a candle in my mouth and a measuring rod in my hand, I went down through a hole large enough for my body and got into a room full of bats, which was only about a meter and a half high. Through another opening that was not blocked I managed to reach the second colonnade, which was full to the ceiling with rubbish. Because all the connecting doors are blocked, the halls can only be seen one at a time, by getting in through the various openings or the holes in the roof, which has already been penetrated in several places."

The French scholars accompanying Napoleon's army also left several traces of their presence in the temple (fig. 24). Above the small door that opens in the western tower of the pylon to the bridge leading to the eastern tower, they carved a narrow rectangle exactly one meter long. At the bottom right is the word "MÈTRE," which refers to the basic unit of measurement of the new metrical system introduced in France in 1795. Directly

Fig. 24: Graffito of the French engineer Legentil, c.1799.

beside it is the name of the man who put the graffito there: "LEGENTIL, INGÉNIEUR FRANÇAIS." The date is given as "AN 8," that is, year eight of the new French Republic (1799). The introduction of the new unit of measurement was four years old, and the French engineer was still so proud of this major achievement that he wanted to announce it even in this remote spot. In another graffito near the one mentioned a soldier of Napoleon's army has given testimony of his devotion and bravery: "Vaincre ou mourir" (Victory or death).

Several Europeans traveled within Egypt in the decades before and after the French expedition and published their impressions, drawings, and later even photographs. They include the Dane Frederik Ludwig Norden (1737–38), the Englishman Richard Pococke (1737–38), the German Carsten Niebuhr (1761–62), the Scotsman David Roberts (1838), and the English photographer Francis Frith (1856–59). Most of them also visited Edfu, and so information about the great temple found its way to Europe.

Mention also has to be made of the multi-talented Vivant Denon, who accompanied the Napoleonic expedition as illustrator and documented a large number of ancient Egyptian monuments as they appeared at the time. It was Denon who recognized the special quality of Edfu and was inspired to write the following description: "This is my third visit to Edfu, and with each visit its temple seems to increase in grandeur. I have come to the conclusion that while that of Dendera may be more artistic in its details, the temple of Edfu is more majestic in its totality. . . . What I have been able to see of the reliefs is perfect to a high degree and reveals a particular feeling for beauty."

In the mid-nineteenth century still far less than half of the reliefs could be seen. The temple was still deeply buried in rubbish and densely occupied by the inhabitants of Edfu. The French writer Gustave Flaubert, who visited Edfu in 1850, has left us a lively account: "The village is situated around the enormous temple and climbs up part of it. Massive pylons, the largest I have ever seen. Inside the pylons several rooms . . . . Wonderful

view from the pylons . . . . Directly beneath you is the village,
with houses covered in straw matting. Everywhere is bustle and
activity: a woman gives water to a donkey from a pumpkin, two
goats in combat ramming each other with their horns. Above, on
the pylon, the names of French soldiers. The temple of Edfu
serves as a public lavatory for the whole village."

Nevertheless, despite these difficult circumstances, French
scholars had already begun to record the temple of Edfu as accu-
rately as possible. They documented it not merely with artists'
renderings but also with architects' drawings, ground plans,
views, and sections. They copied whole sequences of scenes, individual ritual scenes, and hieroglyphs. Even if this was only a frac-
tion of the whole, and full of mistakes and inaccuracies despite
their efforts and care—the temple was buried in the sand, and the
discipline of Egyptology had not yet seen the light of day— it represented the beginning of scientific investigation of the temple of
Edfu, as published in the *Description de l'Égypte* (1809–28).

Karl Richard Lepsius, the German scholar, also visited the
temple of Edfu in order to copy scenes and inscriptions. He was
the director of the Prussian expedition to Egypt (1842–45) and
already a true Egyptologist who could read hieroglyphic texts.
Lepsius had discovered on the outside of the eastern enclosure
wall the great title-deed of the temple and recognized its importance. He wanted to copy it and began the work of clearing away
the high mounds of rubbish from the area. However, he did not
have the resources to complete the work, and so he was not able
to copy much more than the first part of the long text.

The attempts of the first Egyptologists were thus severely
restricted. Until the temple was cleared and cleaned, a comprehensive scientific survey of the architecture and reliefs was
impossible. The temple was cleared shortly afterwards, in 1860,
as a result of the fruitful combination of the energy of the French
Egyptologist Auguste Mariette and the openness of the viceroy of
Egypt, Sa'id, who supported the committed scholar with gener-
ous financial assistance and with all the necessary permits.

Mariette cleared the temple of sand and rubbish, and removed the mud-brick huts, whose inhabitants were relocated. After the work of clearing, visitors to the temple were able to see and appreciate the temple in its almost complete state of preservation for the first time. In 1877, the English writer and amateur Egyptologist Amelia Edwards described the building,

> now standing free in a deep open space, the sides of which are in some places as perpendicular as the quarried cliffs of Silsilis. In the midst of this pit, like a risen God issuing from the grave, the huge building stands before us in the sunshine, erect and perfect. The effect at first sight is overwhelming .... Who enters that gate crosses the threshold of the past, and leaves two thousand years behind him.

In addition to the voices of those admiring the clearance of the temple, there were voices that drew attention to the huge task involved in understanding the abundance of wall decoration. In the fourth edition of his book of popular scholarship (1881), Karl Oppel wrote: "There is a lot to do here for those who wish to study the columns, wall decoration, and suchlike."

A few Egyptologists soon started work in the now freely accessible temple. But Ernst Ritter von Bergmann, Heinrich Brugsch, Johannes Dümichen, Edouard Naville, Karl Piehl, and Jacques de Rougé, who were among the scholars involved, copied only extracts of the scenes and texts. With remarkable perspicacity and understanding, they selected and published some of the most interesting texts. Although these early copies contain a number of errors, they are nevertheless important for modern scholarship, because they reproduce portions of text that, in the meantime, have been partially or totally lost, either through the execution of necessary repair works or through willful destruction by visitors.

In 1876 Maxence de Rochemonteix began the preliminary work of a systematic publication of all scenes and texts of Edfu.

But his working conditions were extremely difficult. He writes: "One of the (temple) rooms served as a kitchen and dining room, the other as bedroom and study, with a bunk from the boat, one or two washing baskets, two light wooden boards for books and papers, four chairs, a table, and a pair of mats . . . used to keep scorpions away . . . . Edfu is very high. My eyes are worn out by the opera glass, my legs by the ladder, my nerves by the heat, and my purse by the boat, whose crew I have to pay, since the boat belongs to me." Light was also a big problem. Most of the temple decoration can be copied only by artificial light, but because there was no electricity then, Rochemonteix had to make do with dim foul-smelling petroleum lamps.

After the regrettably early death of this Egyptologist, the work came to a standstill for some time. Then Émile Chassinat was commissioned to resume the great work. Even though Maxence de Rochemonteix had worked out the plan and made an important initial step, what Chassinat found when he started the work amounted to very little. Just a few sheets of the manuscript were there, and the sheets with the impressions made from the walls had in the meantime become unusable because of the poor storage conditions and the all too frequent transport.

Consequently, Chassinat had to start all over again. In about four decades he copied the inscriptions of the main temple (minus the Mammisi) and published them between 1897 and 1934. There were eight volumes of text, with approximately 3,000 pages in total, two volumes with line drawings, and four volumes of photographs. Between 1984 and 1987 Sylvie Cauville and Didier Devauchelle published a revised second edition of the first two volumes because the first edition contained too many mistakes. The same scholars produced another volume in 1985 with texts and copies of the scenes that had been omitted. Nevertheless, when seen as part of the whole they were only supplements. The magnificent publication of Émile Chassinat had already created a foundation that allowed others to study the Edfu texts more comprehensively than had previously been possible.

The Egyptologists got to work. And, once again, it was detailed work at first, which dealt with individual problems of the difficult writing system and with smaller or larger units of text. The few names that follow stand for many: Hermann Junker, Émile Chassinat, Maurice Alliot, Dimitri Meeks, Adolphe Gutbub, Philippe Derchain, Constant de Wit, Paul Barguet, Dieter Kurth, Jean-Claude Goyon, Sylvie Cauville, Ragnild Finnestad, Philippe Germond. In addition, there are many quotations from Edfu texts scattered throughout various books and academic journal articles.

But also individual studies began to appear, dealing with particular themes, and these were based on the entire textual corpus. Between 1943 and 1945 Herbert Walker Fairman published his ground-breaking work on the writing system of the temple. Maurice Alliot published two volumes in which he reconstructed the performance of the cult. In 1987 Sylvie Cauville published a comprehensive study of the theology of Edfu and in 1997 Penelope Wilson published a study of the vocabulary of the Edfu texts. The time was ripe for a comprehensive translation of all the inscriptions.

I began this work in 1986 by initiating the Edfu Project, which at first was financed by the German Research Council and since 2002 has been part of the program of the Göttingen Academy of Humanities and Sciences. The project has had and continues to have the financial support necessary for research assistants, equipment, and field work at Edfu.

Fieldwork became indispensable after it had become clear from the photos that Émile Chassinat's publication still contained too many mistakes and omissions that severely limited the work of translation. Consequently, the research team travels to Edfu every year to collate Chassinat's copies with the original, to copy more forgotten texts, and to supplement the still incomplete photographic documentation.

Equipment has improved enormously in the two centuries since the first measurements and records were made by the

French expedition. Electric lighting, high-performance tele-
scopes, video and digital cameras, and, above all, computers
make our work considerably easier.

Research assistants are indispensable. A work of this sort is
far beyond the creative power of an individual. Even when the
philological project is finished after decades, study of the temple
will continue indefinitely, because there will still be errors in the
translation despite all our efforts, and there will remain the
never-ending work of interpretation as well as the art-historical
and architectural study of the huge temple complex.

All the scientific work carried out on the temple is interrelat-
ed. Whoever looks at the overall history of the discovery and
study of the temple will realize that the many individuals who
have worked on it, despite various diversions, have proceeded
consistently in response to the demands made by the subject matter itself and guided by a common pattern of intelligence shared
by investigative minds.

There has been a quite different sort of rediscovery of the
Edfu Temple. People come from far away, often from the United
States, in order to worship the god Horus. I once met a group in
the sanctuary as they were about to initiate new members of their
community. The one about to be initiated sat cross-legged in the
great shrine of the sanctuary. The others stood in a devotional
attitude in a circle around the new disciple, dressed in flowing
robes. They swayed gently back and forth, humming in a deep
continuous tone. As I looked on inquiringly, a woman from the
group told me that they had all found direct access to the temple
and god by deep spiritual immersion in the temple area with its
images and signs, intuitively grasping the ancient shrine's holiness
without recourse to the circuitous route of scholarship. As an
Egyptologist, I could only take note of what she said and marvel
at the extent to which the luminous eye of Horus continues to
send forth its rays from Edfu.

The Great Building Inscription of the Edfu Temple: Translation

The King's Temple is Accepted by Horus (1)

Long live (the King with the name) Horus,[1] of divine body, with whom the living Apis Bull became united on the birth bricks, the perfect youth, loved by all, whom his mother caused to appear in glory on the throne of his father, who strikes the foreign countries with his strong arm and seizes with his might, like Ra appearing on the horizon, the Two Ladies (name), who satisfies the Two Lands (Egypt), the strong bull who oversees She-neheh (the Mediterranean Sea?), the King of Upper and Lower Egypt **The Heir of Euergetes II** (Ptolemy X) and his sister and wife, the Ruler and Mistress of the Two Lands, (Cleopatra) **Berenice III**, the two Philometors, beloved of Horus Behdety, the Great God and Lord of Heaven, Ra-Harakhty in the Great Seat (Edfu).

This perfect place, the nome of Horus-Ra (Edfu), is his horizon on earth, is the House of Appearance of His Majesty (Horus of Edfu), is the Great Throne of his Ka, on which he appears (in

---

1   See glossary under 'Royal Titulary.'

the morning) and sets (in the evening), is the Shrine that Protects Khepry of the quickly born (sun-)child, is the place at which his body has been nourished since the First Beginning, is the Chamber *(djerit)* of the Falcon *(djerty)*, is the Ruler's House of the ruler, is the Tomb of the Falcon with the Dappled Plumage (Horus), is the Great Place of the greatest of the gods, is the House of the Strong One of Horus, the strong bull, is the Palace of the Revenger (Horus), who drives the hot-headed (enemies) from the land (Egypt), is the Place of Stabbing of the one who stabs the Wamemti Snake (Apophis), is the Horizon of Eternity and Primeval Hill of the horizon god (Horus), is the Shrine of the divine Winged Disk.

His Majesty (Horus) shines daily, high in the heavens, after he has illuminated the Two Lands (Egypt) with his beauty (light). When Behdety has come down from heaven, he, the lord of the gods, enters his palace, where he is received with hymns of praise by the divine Ennead. All those who live in Mesen (Edfu) rejoice. He sees that Maat is lit up in Edfu as Hathor, the Great One and Mistress of Dendera, and that her handsome son, Harsomtus, beloved of all, has taken his place beside her. When he has recognized that perfection flourishes in his temple and that all the cult therein is according to rule, his heart rejoices. After he has become united with his statue, he praises Ra because of his beloved city. There is jubilation in heaven and rejoicing on earth. The Banks of Horus (Egypt) are in festive mood and the Throne of Horus (Edfu) is in festive joy.

The House of the Falcon (Edfu) rejoices after Horus-Ra has united with the Golden One, the Mistress of Dendera, after the king and the queen have come together while their son sits at their side as king of Upper and Lower Egypt, these, who are the Enduring Ones of Edfu, the kings of Egypt, the Kas of Egypt, who keep the Two Lands of Egypt alive.

After Horus Behdety, the great God and Lord of Heaven, with the Dappled Plumage, who comes forth from the horizon, the King of Upper and Lower Egypt, has seen the Enclosure wall that surrounds his temple as the horizon surrounds the sun-disk, the superb building of which there is no equal, constructed for him by the King of Upper and Lower Egypt **The Heir of Euergetes II** (Ptolemy X), he praises his beloved son for his work and gives him all that is encompassed by his sun-disk when he has appeared as king of Upper and Lower Egypt on the throne of Horus as the first of the living Kas, forever.

The Building History of the Temple

The magnificent Apy revealed himself in heaven as Behdety, the Great God and Lord of Heaven, and made his way to his nome (Edfu). He found his shrine pleasant and took his place on his throne. He looked at this perfect work, constructed for him by his beloved heir, the King of Upper and Lower Egypt **The Heir of Euergetes II**, the Son of Ra **Ptolemy X Alexander I**, beloved of Horus Behdety, the Great God and Lord of Heaven, with the Dappled Plumage, who comes forth from heaven as Ra-Harakhty to his Great Seat (Edfu). He looked at this perfect and splendid monument in Mesen (Edfu), the like of which had never been constructed since the time of the primeval gods, this great wonder without precedent and never there since the time of the gods, this magnificent construction without equal among the temples of Egypt. He passed through this perfect corridor around the work of his predecessors (I' F' and fig. 3): both resemble the horizon, and those who enter them enter heaven.

These are the perfect and excellent monuments created by His Majesty and his forefathers. Their names were carved in them with bronze (tools), so that they might endure on their works, so that they might be thought perfect by their successors, so that their names might be as enduring as their monuments, so that god might be praised because of His Majesty and his work, so that the perfection of those who created him (the predecessors of the King) might be extolled, so that their prestige might be increased even by those who were unable to see them, so that the generations who were unable to know them might worship them, so that their names might be uttered in the Great Seat (Edfu) for millions and millions of years and the (God) with the Dappled Plumage (Horus) might praise them for their deeds, so that their royal office might remain for eternity.

May your hearts rejoice, you Kings of Upper and Lower Egypt, Royal Priest (?) and Semer-priests of the Great Seat (Edfu), you Hatia-priests and overseers of the divine servants in the temples, you great Wab-priests of Egypt, you great scholars and writers from Elephantine to the Mediterranean coast. Come downstream from the south and sail upstream from the north. Disembark at the Throne of Ra (Edfu) and ascend to the shrine of the divine Winged Disk, to kiss the ground before the (God) with the Dappled Plumage. Process through this perfect corridor, hasten to visit all four corners of the Great Seat, and hear about the great monuments constructed by His Majesty in Edfu and also about the works of his fathers and mothers.

The Great Seat of Ra (the main fabric of the temple) was built within the Enclosure wall, like the horizon of heaven. In front of it is a Pronaos, which stretches from the eastern mountain to the western mountain. It is like heaven with the Bas of the gods. It is broader than the temple both right and left. Its height reaches above the first chamber of the Naos (plan and fig. 3). Columns in the form of papyrus plants and date-palms (fig. 6 and fig. 20) support the heaven of its roof, just as the four goddesses support the heaven of the world.

There is an Offering Court with surrounding columns in front of it (H'), as light as the sky-goddess Nut when she has given birth to the daylight. There is a Pylon (K') in front of it, right and left (with its two towers), like the divine sisters Isis and Nephthys who raise up the sun.

Specification of the beautiful days on which the foundation of the temple was begun, of the excellent months in which the measuring rope was extended, of the successful years in which the work was started, and of the Senut-festivals in which its measures were made; list of the Kings of Upper Egypt before whom the foundation trenches were dug and of the Kings of Lower Egypt who unrolled the cord, the rulers whose names are carved in it (the temple), [each of them bequeathing the (royal) heritage] to his son:

This beautiful day in the 10th [regnal year], day 7 of the month Epiphi, in the time of the Majesty of the Son of Ra **Ptolemy III Euergetes I** (fig. 25), was the day of the Senut-festival,[2] when the measurements (of the temple) were laid out on the ground. The first of all Senut-festivals on the occasion of extending the measuring rope at the foundation of the Great Seat of Ra-Harakhty (Edfu), of the foundation of the Throne Seat of the Protector of his Father (Edfu). The King himself and the goddess Seshat, the great one, established the plan of the First Shrine (Edfu). The correct position of the temple chambers was determined by the gods of the creator-word together with the Lord of the Heden Plant (Thoth). The Khnum gods began to form, Ptah fashioned, and the first group of primeval gods broke out in jubilation round about. The Shrine of the Divine Winged Disk (the Naos of Edfu) was completed, the Mesen of the Falcon of the Golden One (Horus) was finished by the 10th regnal year, 3rd month of the season of Shemu, day 7 in the time of the King of Upper and Lower Egypt, Son of

Fig. 25: Ptolemy III
Euergetes I.

Ra **Ptolemy IV Philopator**[3] (fig. 26), after a total of 25 years. The interior walls were decorated wonderfully with reliefs, with the

2   Corresponds to 23 August 237 B.C.
3   17 August 212 B.C.

Fig. 26: Ptolemy IV Philopator.

full titulary of His Majesty, with the figures of the gods and images of the goddesses together with all the splendor of the One Who Creates Magnificence (Edfu). Its main gates and the double doors of its chambers were completed by year 16 of His Majesty.

Then trouble broke out. There was an uprising of rebels in Upper Egypt, and work on the Throne Seat of the Gods (Edfu) was suspended. [The rebellion?] in the south [lasted?] until year 19 of the King of Upper and Lower Egypt **The Heir of Philopator,** Son of Ra **Ptolemy V, blessed,** Epiphanes, the strong one, the king (fig. 27), who put an end to the trouble completely. His name, too was recorded in the temple.

In regnal year 5, day 1 of the month Shef-bedet (the first month of the season of Peret) of his beloved son, the King of Upper and Lower Egypt **The Heir of Epiphanes,** the Son of Ra **Ptolemy VI, blessed**[4] (fig. 28), the main gate of Great of Victory (Edfu) was installed, together with the double doors of its chapels. Work was resumed in the House of the Strong One (Edfu) in year 30 of this king: the tracing out of the inscriptions (with ink) and the carving with bronze tools, the embellishing of its walls with gold, the laying on of the colors, the completion of its (wooden) door leaves (?), the mounting (?) of its pivots with perfect bronze, the carving of the holes for its bolts with bronze tools, the gilding of the doors, thus completing Mesen (the temple of Edfu) in superb workmanship executed by the best craftsmen by year 28,

4   3 February 176 B.C.

Fig. 27: Ptolemy V Epiphanes.   Fig. 28: Ptolemy VI Philometor.

month 4 of the season of Shemu, day 18 of His Majesty, the King of Upper and Lower Egypt **The Heir of Epiphanes**, Son of Ra **Ptolemy VIII, blessed**, Euergetes II (fig. 29)[5] and his consort, the Ruler and Mistress of the Two Lands, **Cleopatra II**. The whole work took 95 years, from extending the measuring rope to the Entering the Temple Festival, in which the House of Eternity (Edfu) was handed over by His Majesty to its owner, Horus of Behdety, the Great God and Lord of Heaven.

There was a great festival of drunkenness, without equal since the foundation of the earth until now. As day began, very early in the morning, Edfu was inundated with all good things, millions and hundreds of thousands of delicious foods; [bread and beer] were abundant and immeasurable, there was plenty of cattle and fowl, Iua- and Wenedju-cattle that made the altars festive, with fat geese

5   10 September 142 B.C.

Fig. 29: Ptolemy VIII Euergetes II.

as burnt offerings, with myrrh, incense, and ointment [on the glowing charcoal], so that the sky over Mesen (Edfu) was no longer visible. The ground swam in the Green Horus Eye (wine), wine from Shefit and Imet. The Royal Priest and the Semer-priests attended in their festival garments and the temples were well-equipped. The inhabitants of Dendera joined the inhabitants of Edfu, men and women together, drunk with wine and anointed with Tishepes-oil, with garlands around their necks. (Horus) Behdety displayed himself in his processional bark [like] his sun-disk that rises in the eastern mountains. He accepted his Great Seat (Edfu), his magnifi-cent horizon, and entered his house full of festival joy. It will endure with him and will elevate His Majesty from this day to the end of eternity. Mesen (Edfu) was inscribed on the outside with the titulary of His Majesty.

This beautiful occasion in regnal year 30, month 2 of the season of Shemu, day 9,[6] on the day of the union of Osiris with the left eye of Ra (the moon), was the day of the Senut-festival in the month of Payni (2nd of the season of Shemu), on which the measuring rope was laid perfectly at the foundation of the Pronaos of the First-of-the-Temples-of-Egypt (Horus of Edfu). This Heaven of the Lord of Heaven (Edfu) was completed in regnal year 46, month 4 of the season of Shemu, day 18,[7] a total of 16 years, 2 months and 10 days

---

6   2 July 140 B.C.
7   5 September 124 B.C.

from the foundation of the horizon (Pronaos) to the festival of Entering the Pronaos. The great festival of drunkenness for the marvelous Pronaos was exactly the same as the beautiful feast for this house (the Naos). The titulary of His Majesty was carved in its walls, dating from his regnal year 48 to the end of his days. In regnal year 54 of this king, month 2 of the season of Shemu, day 11,[8] after the foundation trenches of the Enclo-sure wall, the Great Courtyard and the Pylon had been excavated and the cord had been loosened in all of them, the falcon opened his wings towards heaven (the king died). His eldest son appeared on the throne and his

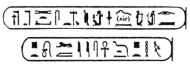

Fig. 30: Ptolemy IX Soter II.

name was engraved on the outside of the Pronaos of the temple as King of Upper and Lower Egypt **The Heir of Euergetes II**, [Son of Ra **Ptolemy IX** (fig. 30) . . . (his younger brother ascended the throne) . . .] and he took [the office of king (?)] in peace. His name was carved on the Enclosure wall of Mesen (Edfu) as King of Upper and Lower Egypt **The Heir of Euergetes II**, Son of Ra **Ptolemy X Alexander I** until he hastened off to Punt (died). Then his elder brother (Ptolemy IX) regained possession of Egypt and he became king of Egypt once again.[9]

O you Kings of Upper and Lower Egypt who have created these monuments, you falcons who have opened your wings (died),

8   28 June 116 B.C.
9   The temple was completed on 5 December 57 B.C. under Ptolemy XII and his daughters (*Edfou* V, 304, 11ff.).

may your Bas always be divine in heaven with Ra and your corpses
enduring in the underworld. May you walk freely through the Hall
of the Two Maat and be justified before Osiris. May your images be
indestructible on earth and your heirs be secure on your thrones.

Horus Behdety, the Great God and Lord of Heaven, shines in
the sky and looks at his house. He praises his beloved son, the King
of Upper and Lower Egypt **The Heir of Euergetes II**, Son of Ra
Ptolemy IX, and he has made him secure on his throne forever.

The King's Temple is Accepted by Horus (2)

Long live (the King with the names) Golden Horus of strong will,
loved by the gods of Egypt, ruler and lord of the two Uraeus-
snakes, who entered Egypt in peace, his soldiers rejoicing and gods
and goddesses protecting him, to whom numerous Sed-festivals
were given by Ptah, the father of the gods, to whom the kingdom
of Ra-Atum was given and power and strength of Amun, the lord
of Maat who realizes Maat, who strengthens the laws like Thoth,
the Twice Great, the Son of Ra **Ptolemy X Alexander I** (fig. 31),
with his sister and consort, the ruler and mistress of the Two Lands
(Cleopatra) **Berenice III**, the two Philometors, beloved of Horus
Behdety, the Great God and Lord of Heaven, the Falcon of the
Golden-One (Hathor), the Lord of the Throne Seat (Edfu).

Isis raised her Horus in Throne Seat (Edfu), and so arose
Throne Seat of Horus as its (Edfu's) true name. The nome is also
called Djeba ('Place of Punishment'), because this is where Horus
punished Seth. It (the temple of Edfu) is also called Throne of
Horus, since he (Horus) took his place on the throne, and also the
House of the Ruler of the ruler among the Gods with the Strong
Forehead, [10] and also Great Place of the greatest among the gods,
and also Mesen of the Lord of Mesen, which is in Upper Egypt
like his Mesen Tjaru in Lower Egypt, and also the Seat of

---

10   "Ruler among the Gods with the Strong Forehead," "greatest among the
     gods," "the one who stabs," "the quickly born child," and "Great
     Falcon" are all designations of Horus.

Fig. 31: Ptolemy X Alexander I.

Stabbing of the one who stabs the evil ones, also the House of the
Strong One of the (warrior) Harsiese, and the Great Protected
(Shrine) of the quickly born child (who is to be protected), also
the Chamber *(djerit)* of the Falcon *(djerty)*, Lord of the Falcon
Gods *(djertyu)*, and also the House of the Falcon of the Great
Falcon with his wings protecting the inhabitants of his city.

   Which nome can be compared to his nome, the nome of This
One, the falcon, the lord of the temple? The protective gods
ensure the protection of their shrine, and his image is [engraved]
on this wall that surrounds its lord protectively. He can attack millions, but nobody can attack him.

   This holy seat has been built in the most excellent manner: it
resembles the heaven with the sun disk in it. Horus Behdety, the
Great God and Lord of Heaven, shines in the firmament, in order
to look at his temple. He protects his beloved son, the Son of Ra
Ptolemy X Alexander I, because of this monument of his, while
he is enduring as a falcon on the palace façade (throne), as the
first of the Kas of the living, forever.

The Description of the Temple

(Horus), the falcon of the Golden One (Hathor), revealed himself in heaven as Behdety, (the God) with the Dappled Plumage, and he accepted his city. After uniting himself with his temple, His Majesty took his place on his throne. He contemplated the remarkable work, the miracle, built by his son and successor, the King of Upper and Lower Egypt **The Heir of Euergetes II**, Son of Ra **Ptolemy X Alexander I**, beloved of Horus Behdety, the Great God and Lord of Heaven, the Lord of Mesen, with the Dappled Plumage, who comes forth from the horizon, the magnificent Apy in the temples of Egypt, the great god, who is greater than all gods, (contemplating) the perfect and magnificent monument surrounding his temple (the Enclosure wall), outside in front of the work of his (the king's) predecessors: the length of this wall is 240 cubits, its width 90 cubits, its height to the top 20 cubits, and the thickness of its foundations 5 cubits.

These are the monuments created by His Majesty and his predecessors, like the horizon of heaven, and here are the details of their chapels and the list of their halls, the specification of their dimensions and of their columns, the knowledge of their gates, the individual description of their staircases and information about the number of their roof chapels, details of their doors, which are opened therein towards every place they are intended to lead to, the description of their walls, which have been decorated most perfectly by the master craftsmen of the House of Life. All the decoration of them was carried out in accordance with the writings; its floor was laid as it should be. All its heavens (ceilings) are covered with stars, and Horus Behdety, in the perfect form of the divine Apy, shines among them, protected by his two Uraeus-snakes. Each god (in a ritual scene) is in his place, each goddess in her position; the king wears his crowns, performs his duty, and makes offerings. The gods are in their chapels and the Divine Ennead in their hall; the Hidden One (Osiris) is hidden in the Hidden Seat (Edfu as crypt), and the gods of heaven are in their right place above his (Osiris's) horizon. The protector snakes and the combat-ready demons are on duty. The papyrus rolls are in their place (E'), as it should be, and each ritual takes place where it is supposed to.

This here (the Naos) is the Great Seat of Ra-Harakhty, the Throne of (Horus) the Protector of his Father. It is 105 cubits long and 63 cubits wide. How wonderful is its height, with 22 2/3 cubits. The Mesenet room (I) is the first chapel on its central axis and the great throne of the (God) with the Dappled Plumage (Horus). Maat is at his side as Hathor, the Great One, in his secret shrine that is located in Mesenet. The chapel is 8 1/3 cubits long and 6 2/3 cubits wide. Its walls are decorated with the Divine Ennead of Mesenet, as they appear in their true form before Horus and Hathor.

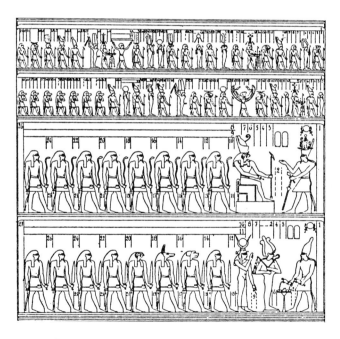

Fig. 32: Room G, north wall: ". . . and decorated with the protector gods . . . ."

The chapel Shetjit (G), to the right (west) of it and decorated with the protector gods (fig. 32), is 7 5/6 cubits by 6 2/3
cubits. The House of the Prince (Osiris; H) is behind it
(Shetjit), opening on to it, and measuring 6 2/3 (cubits) by the
same (6 2/3). The chapel known as the Inner Part of Shetjit (F)
is to the southwest of it, a square room of 8 cubits (on every
side). These are the palaces of Iun (Osiris) in Behdet. His
forms have been carved on the walls of the three chambers.
The two weeping and mourning women, the two sisters, protect him; they are the two kites, Isis and Nephthys, are the ones
who transfigure his Ka. The four Asebet goddesses protect the
bier. The four Anubis gods, the four door-keepers of the
underworld, [. . .], the sharp-eyed protective gods. The gods of
the underworld, who do not leave their districts, are jointly
responsible for his protection. Horus the Protector of his
Father protects him. Thoth the Great One reads the festival ritual for him. The gods of Behdet, the Children of Harakhte, the
living Ba of Ra in the midst of his children and the underworld
gods, who guard the nome [and] his [towns], are in their place,
and watch over him.

The chambers Throne of the Gods (E) and House of Cloth
(D; fig. 33) contain an inventory of the nome. Each chamber is 8
cubits (on every side). All together, there are [five] chambers [to
the right of it (chamber I)], as it has been laid down since the
beginning of time.

The chamber House of the Leg (J), which belongs to Khonsu
of Edfu, is to the left of it (chamber I). The Chapel of Hathor (K)
is also to the left of it and serves as its magazine. The Seat of the
First Festival is above it (on the temple roof), its façade facing
south, [. . .] inscribed with the rites of the Seat of the First
Festival. . . . [. . . (the chamber Throne of Ra (L) . . . in] their
forms as Divine Ennead of this nome.

The chamber Behdet (M) is to the left of it, and contains the
image of the goddess Mehit and the Divine Ennead, who watch
over Osiris. The god Shu is there as north wind, in order to

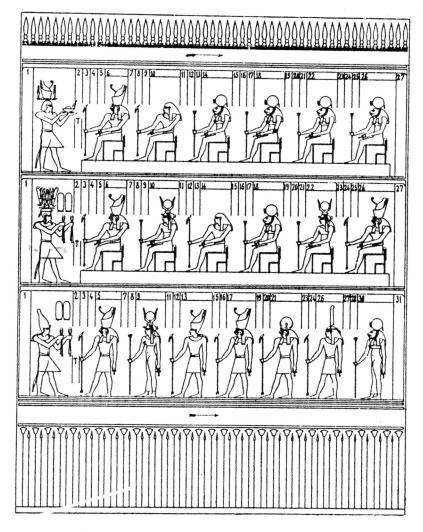

Fig. 33: Room D, south wall: ". . . House of Cloth . . . ."

Fig. 34: Sanctuary (A), east wall: ". . . Revealing the God's face . . . ."

unite himself with Osiris's nostrils, as is his duty in the Horizon
of Eternity (the tomb), together with Tefnut as flame in order to
burn the enemies of Osiris, as she does in Areq-heh when she is
the goddess Menet, the Eye of Ra with the fear-inspiring pupil
(and at the same time) the goddess Sekhmet, the Great One, the
Mistress of all Sekhmet goddesses [. . .].

All together, there are four (chapels) to the left of it (chamber
I), as is right. Their dimensions are the same as those opposite.
Their doors all open on to the corridor, which is 3 5/6 cubits wide.
The Enduring Ones, the Ancestor Gods, and the Divine Ennead
of the nome are visible on each wall in the corridor.

The Great Seat (the sanctuary; A) in the midst of the chapels
and surrounded by the corridor mentioned, measures 19 5/6 cubits
by 10 1/3 cubits. The doors of the corridor are to its right and left,
and give access to the surrounding chapels. The processional
bark of the (God) with the Dappled Plumage (Horus), his

Fig. 35: Sanctuary (A), west wall: ". . . Burning Incense
for the Processional Bark."

magnificent (portable) shrine next to it, and his great Naos of
black stone that is next to both of them, they are wonderful to
behold. His Seat of the Talon in heaven, his Dwelling on earth, his
Throne Seat in the temple heaven (three names of the sanctuary)
is inscribed with the Divine Ennead of the nome. The rituals of
the Lord are dedicated to him (Horus Behdety): *Revealing the
God's face* (fig. 34), *Offering Maat to its Creator (Ra)*, and *Burning
Incense for the Processional Bark* (fig. 35).

The Central Hall (N) is in front of the Sanctuary. Dwelling
Place of the Gods and Birth House of the Strong Horus are its
names. It is 23 ²/3 by 9 cubits. The (portable) shrines of the gods,
whose beauty is praised, are kept here; the Divine Ennead of
Mesen is depicted on its walls.

The House of Min (O) is to the right of it (the Central Hall),
a square of 8 cubits (on every side), containing the god Min with
his crowns and in his ritual scenes (fig. 36).

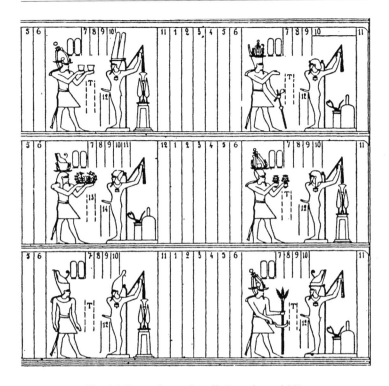

Fig. 36: Room O, south wall: ". . . the god Min
with his crowns and in his ritual scenes."

The Court of the Food Offerings Altar (Q; fig. 37) is to the
left of it (the Central Hall) and in it is its Wabet (P), each one a
square of 8 cubits (on every side). Here ointment, clothing, and
protective amulets are offered to provide the god with his finery.
His Majesty is purified with his natron-balls and his nemset-jars,
so that his Ba may unite with his image. The heaven belongs to its
lord and to the forms in which he appears, Ra having been
equipped with his Weeya-boat at midday, while the Mesketet-boat
in the evening, and the Mandjet-boat in the morning carry

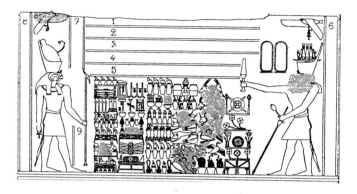

Fig. 37: Court Q, south wall: "The Court of
the Food Offerings Altar . . . ."

Khepry and Atum, one at sunrise and one at sunset (fig. 38). The
king praises his Ka and his Ba, kills his enemies, and provides his
house with bread, meat, and beer.

The Offering Table Hall (R) is in front of them, with a
length of 25 cubits and a width of 8 cubits. It is decorated on its
inside walls with the rites of the divine offering and with all the
cult actions prescribed for it.

On the east and west sides of it (the Offering Table Hall)
there is a staircase by which it is possible to *rise* and *set*: this
(*sun-*)god will ascend (to the temple-roof) via the eastern staircase (U), together with his Uraeus-snake, the Great One, in
order to see his sun-disk (in the sky), and with his Divine
Ennead following him in order to unite with his Ba (the sun) on
the day of the New Year Festival, after having descended and
entered (in the previous year) his temple chamber, by the staircase on the west side (T), accompanied by his great Uraeus-
snake, the Mistress of Dendera (Hathor), and his Divine
Ennead, each one in his place, having returned satisfied and
taken his place in his horizon (temple), thus fulfilling his circuit,
together with them (his fellow-gods), and for eternity.

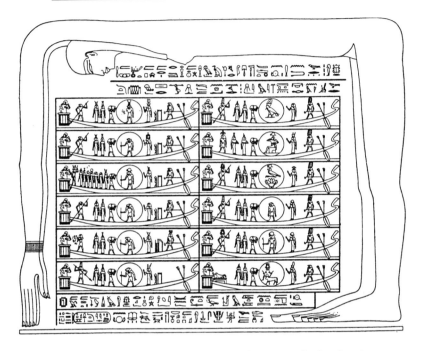

Fig 38: Room P, ceiling: "The heaven belongs to its lord and to the
forms in which he appears, Ra having been equipped
with his Weeya-boat at mid-day. . . ."

The flight of stairs on the west side measures 60 by [2?]
cubits. The eastern staircase measures 10 by 8; it has a small door
in it that opens on to its Wabet; all together, there are three doors
in it (to rooms Q, R, and W). There is a room (S) to the right of
it (the Offering Table Hall), measuring 10 by 9, into which the
flight of stairs on the right leads.

The Great Hall (W) is in front of it: it has twelve columns,
great supports, wonderful to behold. The hall is 37 (cubits) long
and 26 wide. Its walls are most perfectly decorated: it is called
Place of Pleasure. It is also known as Place of Joy and Place of

Enjoyment of Ra and Horus, for it resembles the Chemmis (papyrus thicket) of their son (Harsomtus).

There is a room (Z) to the west, 10 (cubits) by 4: it is completely decorated with the works of the Lord of the Ointment-workshop.

To the south is the Connecting Room (A'), 13 ¹/₃ (cubits long) and 4 cubits wide. Its door opens on to the above-mentioned hall (W) and gives access to the Pure Corridor. Its walls are decorated with ritual scenes depicting the water libations and the spells for blessing them, which takes place there.

All this is on the left side of it (the Hall; W): another door of the staircase, which opens on to it, so that one can reach the temple roof in order to let the clothes become light (in the New Year Festival) and to visit all the (roof-)chapels.

Moreover, there is a door of the Connecting Room (Y), south of it, opening on to the Corridor just as on the right (western) side. This room has the perfect dimensions of 7 (cubits) by 4 and contains all rituals for the presentation of the food offerings.

The Treasury (B') is to the south of it (the Connecting Room), opens on to it and measures 11 cubits by 4. It is the Perfect Seat for gold, silver, precious stones, and protective amulets.

The Pronaos (the Outer Hypostyle Hall; C') comes after it (the Hall W), which is higher than the rooms mentioned and wider on the right and left sides: it is 40 [+x] cubits by 36, with a total height of 30 cubits, and it is most perfectly carved on its inside with reliefs. The House of Morning (D') and the Library (E') are on the right and left sides of it. There is a small door in it, facing eastwards. There are 18 perfect columns that support the [horizon (the ceiling)], just as the sky is supported under the Winged Scarab.

This Corridor, which is pure and leads around all this (F'–I' and fig. 3), is within the wall, which is connected with the Pylon (K'). It is 113 cubits long and 90 cubits wide, up to the small doors that are located in it on the right and left sides of the Pronaos. There are four doors in it (F'– I'). Details of the places on to which the doors open: one leads eastwards (I'–J'1) and is used by the Aqi-priests when they come back from the Sacred Lake to perform their duty; it is used to bring out offerings released (for consumption), in order to hand them out to the overseers of the chapels of the (God) with the Dappled Plumage (Horus); another one, a miraculous work, leads to the Pure Well (I'–J'2), [. . .], to the Pure Magazine and to the Slaughterhouse of Horus of the choicest cuts of meat, to get fresh pure water for the temple, and for the divine offering to the Falcon at the appropriate time; two more (doors) open right and left, and they are sited in the Pronaos and lead into the Offering Court (H').

This Court, which is in front of the Pronaos, is like that: it is broader than the Pronaos on the one side and the other. It measures 90 cubits from south to north by 80 from west to east, corresponding to the inner measurement of the wall that surrounds all this. There are 32 columns around it and they make a corridor that resembles this Nest of the Falcon. It (the court) is the perfect palace of Nut and its name is: Place in which Seftekh (Apophis) is Defeated, the Enemy of Harakhte. Its walls are appropriately decorated in accordance with what has been found in the ancient writings.

All together, there are four doors on its west and east sides to allow the multitudes to come in and go out. One of them (H'J'1') is magnificently decorated and situated opposite the Door of the Golden One (Hathor), the Mistress of Dendera, and it is her perfect way to enter her house to unite with her image in the Sanctuary, and (also the way) to proceed to her barge to make her way (in procession) to Behdet at the appropriate time.

Two Pylon towers (K'), 120 (cubits long), stand in front of the court. They are 60 (cubits) high up to the top, and it is the case that each one is 21 cubits wide, on the right and left sides. Their façade has been decorated in accordance with the texts and all instructions to ward off the foreigners. There are numerous treasuries built into them and two doors leading into the Offering Court (H'). One of them, in the eastern Pylon, also leads to the Well of Moistening. All together there are six doors in this court, including those in the wonderful Pylon towers.

Between the Pylon towers is a large decorated gate, 26 $^2/_3$ (cubits) by 10; its perfect height from head to foot is 40 cubits. Its flagpoles are of conifer wood, reach up to heaven, and are covered with Asiatic copper (bronze); they are the two sisters Isis and Nephthys, who protect the Prince of the White Crown (Osiris) and watch over the Ruler of the Temples of Egypt (Horus). Two large solid obelisks stand before them and pierce those clouds of heaven.

This perfect house is surrounded on all four sides by an Enclosure wall (J'), its kingdom is the kingdom of Ra. Its perfect façade shines to the south. There is nothing on earth that can compare with it.

Its perfect doors from genuine conifer wood are covered with Asiatic copper (bronze). Its door-bolts and the frames of its bolt-openings (from sheet copper?) are perfect; all the lions (of the bolts) are ready to act against the foreigners. Its great doors repel the enemies and its walls keep out the foes.

There is much beautiful cult equipment in it, made from silver, gold, and precious stones.

When its perfect lord sees this temple, his heart rejoices, (the heart of) Horus Behdety, the Great God and Lord of Heaven. When its beautiful mistress (Hathor) sees it, she rejoices, the Great One, the Lady of Dendera. They find that there is purity and perfect order in it and excellent priests therein. They praise Ra for their perfect city Throne Seat of Horus (Edfu), the Mistress and Lady of the cities, and they elevate Throne Seat (Edfu) with millions of years, eternal and indestructible forever. They protect their beloved son (the king) because of his monument and they allow his image to endure on earth, the image of the King of Upper and Lower Egypt **The Heir of Euergetes II**, the Son of Ra **Ptolemy X Alexander I**, whose Ka is granted power and strength on the Throne of Horus, at the head of the living, forever.

Glossary

Abydos Capital of the eighth Upper Egyptian nome and most important cult-site of the god Osiris in Upper Egypt.

Amun Principal god of Thebes, with many other cult places in Egypt. Amun (also Amun-Ra) was regarded, among other things, as God of Creation and Lord of *Maat*.

Ancestor Gods These are probably the predecessors of gods who 'die' annually and are reborn. In the case of the sun-god Horus, these are the annual suns of his previous existence. At Edfu there were even tombs of such primeval gods (see also *Dendera*)

Anubis Jackal-headed god of the dead, responsible for the proper burial and thus also the mummification of the body. Anubis was also a guard at the entrance to the underworld who led the deceased into the kingdom of the dead. In the Osiris mysteries he took charge of the nocturnal watches over the dead body of Osiris.

Apis Memphite god in the form of a bull. There was a cult of the living Apis bull and a cult of the dead Apis bull.

Apophis Arch-enemy of the sun in the form of a snake, who wished to prevent the sun-god from crossing the sky—in essence Apophis is the enemy of light. At Edfu he was hated like Seth.

Apy "The One Who Travels (Across the Sky)," a name of the sun-god in his form as winged sun-disk and winged scarab. The winged sun-disk is also the emblem of (Horus) Behdeti, which is depicted on the lintels of almost every temple and shrine.

Aqi-priests A group of priests whose name is possibly derived from the word *aq*, meaning 'to enter.'

Areq-heh A name of the necropolis of Abydos.

Asebet Protective goddess of Ra and Osiris. At Edfu four of these goddesses appear in the form of standing hippopotamuses (similar to the goddess Thoeris), each with a torch in hand.

Atum Principal god of Heliopolis. Creator god, first of the Ennead, who created himself, then produced the first divine couple, Shu and Tefnut, by masturbation or spitting. As sun-god, Atum embodies the evening sun and as such is the counterpart of Khepry, the god of the morning sun. The combination of Khepry, Ra, and Atum embraces the complete 24-hour solar cycle.

Ba 'Ba' and 'Ka' are untranslatable words, but a comparison of the two with a plant may give an approximate idea of their meaning. The 'Ka' corresponds to the root. The 'Ba' corresponds to the stem, the leaf, and the flower. The 'Ka' gives the living being the support necessary for survival, embodies the vital force that is always in need of nourishment, and acts as the basic element that constantly generates new life. The 'Ba' embodies the ability of the living being to manifest itself and to move. And so, for example, the 'Ba' of a human being has the form of bird with a human head, or the sun is called the 'Ba' of the sun-god Ra, or after death someone is said to "go to his Ka." When the body is created, the 'Ka' is also created at the same time, like a second body. The 'Ka' accompanies its owner and protects him.

Behdet A name of Edfu itself and the Sacred Precinct of Edfu (on the latter see also *Dendera*).

Behdety A name of Horus of Edfu, "The One from (the Town of) Behdet" (see also *Horus Behdety*).

Birth bricks Two bricks on which the squatting woman giving birth places her feet.

Busiris Capital of the ninth Lower Egyptian nome, most important cult site of Osiris in Lower Egypt.

Chemmis Place near Buto in the Western Delta, where Horus spent his youth among the papyrus thickets, protected from the persecution of Seth. The temple halls, supported by papyrus columns, are compared to the papyrus thickets of Chemmis.

Crypt Hidden chamber in the temple, often underground, but frequently also in the upper parts of the temple. Place where cult statues and ritual equipment were kept.

Cubit Linear measure of approximately 52 centimeters.

(The God with the) Dappled Plumage An epithet of the falcon-shaped Horus of Edfu, also used of other deities who appear as a falcon.

Dendera A town approximately 180 kilometers to the north of Edfu (see fig. 4), which was closely associated with Edfu in religious terms. Hathor, the principal goddess, visited her consort, Horus, twice a year during the months of Paophi and Epiphi. Together they made their way to the graves of the Primeval Gods of Behdet, the Sacred Precinct situated approximately 12 kilometers to the southwest of the temple. The rites performed there in the month of Epiphi during the course of a fourteen-day festival (depicted on the dado of the south wall of the great court) had a comprehensive regenerating effect on gods, human beings, and nature.

Door of the Golden One This is a name of the door of the Ramesside pylon, which is situated outside the enclosure wall of the temple of Edfu, in its southeast corner just behind the eastern wing of the Pylon. On the occasion of her visit to Edfu, Hathor comes out of this door and after a few meters reaches the door H'J'1' in the enclosure wall, in order to enter the great court.

Elephantine Island near Aswan. Capital of the first Upper Egyptian nome (see fig. 4).

Ennead Originally a community of nine gods worshipped at Heliopolis, consisting of four generations: Atum; Shu and Tefnut; Geb and Nut; Osiris, Seth, Isis, and Nephthys. In the course of time, enneads were formed at other cult sites, which did not always limit themselves to nine. In temples of the Greco-Roman period it is often a designation for any group of gods, such as a group of primeval gods, protective gods, or the retinue of the principal god.

Epiphanes Title of Ptolemy V: 'the (God) Who Appears.'

Euergetes Title of Ptolemies III and VIII: "the Beneficent (God)."

Eye The sun and the moon were regarded as the eyes of a divinity who had cosmic importance. Both eyes are described in the texts with their numerous qualities. They can have as many names as qualities, e.g., 'the Living One,' 'the Shining One,' 'the Whole One.' The periodic disappearance and reappearance of the eyes of the sun and the moon have been interpreted in the myths. Among these latter is the myth of the Distant Goddess (Hathor, Sekhmet, Tefnut, and so on, who travel between the winter and summer solstices as the Eye of Ra, that is, the Eye of the Sun), the Books of the Day- and Night-Journey of the Sun God and the myths of the Eye of the Moon, cut into pieces by Seth and restored to wholeness by Thoth. The sound and intact Eye of Horus was especially significant, namely as the essence of all good offerings. Hence the description of wine, for example, in the offering scenes as the 'Green Eye of Horus' or milk as the 'White Eye of Horus.' Moreover, the Eyes were equated with the Two Crowns. As the Wedjat Eye (Intact Eye), the Eye of Horus possessed great protective power. Copies of it in faience and other materials were considered effective amulets.

Falcon of the Golden One Horus in a particular relationship to Hathor the Golden One (her son and as such the local manifestation of Harsiese?). Frequently equated with Harsiese and Horus Behdety. Many writings of his name also point to the meaning 'Falcon of Gold.'

Flagpoles Four of them were once attached to the façade of the pylon. They represented Isis and Nephthys. Ancient representations (from the Nineteenth Dynasty) show that the flagpoles towered above the pylon and that colored flags were attached to the top of them.

Gemehsu Falcon A bird of prey. Designation of various gods, especially at Edfu of the god Horus as a falcon.

Goddesses supporting the heaven Four goddesses who support the 'roof' of the Egyptian cosmic building: Khyt in the east, Ahayet in the south, Fayet in the west, and Tuayet in the north.

Gods of the Creation Word In ancient Egyptian, *Djaisu*. They came into being out of the mouth of the creator god, as his utterances. As such, they gave life, by means of speech, to the most important elements of creation.

Hall of the Two Maat Room in the underworld for the Judgment of the Dead, to which everyone was subjected. The heart of the dead person was tested on a set of scales to see if it had the weight of *Maat*, that is to say, if it was good, just, and truthful. The chief judge was mostly Osiris.

Hapy The god of the Nile, worshipped particularly as the bringer of the annual flood, on which the fertility of the fields depended.

Harakhty See under *Ra-Harakhty*.

Harsiese *Horus the son of Isis*, to which the epithet "the son of Osiris" is often added, is the Horus of the Osiris myth. In his youth he was threatened by Seth, but nevertheless succeeded in ascending the throne of his father as legally entitled heir. At Edfu he was regarded as a particularly combative god and was very often equated with Horus Behdety.

Harsomtus the Child Son of Hathor of Dendera and Horus of Edfu. Another son of this couple was Ihy. If the two are distinguished from each other, Ihy is assigned to Dendera, and Harsomtus to Edfu.

Hathor of Dendera Principal goddess of Dendera, at Edfu the consort of Horus Behdety, but also his mother and daughter.

Hathor was also regarded as the Eye of the sun god as well as his Uraeus-snake. She assumed characteristics of other goddesses, especially Isis and Maat; frequently she was also identified with Sekhmet, the ferocious lioness, whose anger had to be placated.

Horizon Properly speaking, the horizon as place of the rising and setting of the sun. By extension, any place where there is a solar god, e.g., the temple as earthly dwelling place of the god, and finally the tomb, which was considered a place of (daily) rebirth.

The Horizontal One A name of the sun-god. At Edfu often used for Harakhty, Horus Behdety, and Ra.

Horus Behdety The official name of the principal god and lord of the temple of Edfu. Apart from this primary name, the god also has many other names, as many in fact as he has characteristics. As Horus, he was the guarantor of Egyptian kingship: the reigning king was his representative on earth. The theologians of Edfu also found for their god a place in the myths already widespread in Egypt since antiquity, and in these myths Horus Behdety assumes the role of helper and protector. Thus, he fights for his father Ra, when at the end of the year he is weak and threatened by his enemies; he protects Harsiese, the son of Osiris and Isis, whom Seth wants to kill in order to steal his inheritance.

House of Life A building usually attached to the temple, where theological texts were composed, copied, and kept. It also functioned as a place of training and the performance of rituals designed to keep the world going. A theological and scholarly center, whose significance went far beyond the temple itself.

House of the Morning A small room (D'), set in the façade of the pronaos (C'). Ideally, the king, usually represented by the Royal Priest, was purified there every morning by pouring water over him in order to prepare him for the daily performance of his priestly duty. In reality it was perhaps a statue of the king that received the rites as a substitute.

Ihy See under *Harsomtus the Child*.

Isis Sister and consort of Osiris. She brought up her son Horus in the Delta marshes of Chemmis and protected him from the persecution of Seth, who had killed his father and wanted to rob Horus of his inheritance. As Isis supported her son, she also played a major part in reviving Osiris. This made her into the paragon of the loyal wife and caring mother.

Isis and Nephthys Daughters of Geb and Nut. In the morning they lift the sun up into the sky. They are identified with the two towers of the pylon and the flagpoles that stand in front of the pylon. They protect, transfigure, and revive their brother Osiris. They were also known to appear in the form of two birds (probably kites).

Ka See *Ba*.

Khepry God of the morning sun, hence also creator and primeval god. Mostly appears as the morning form of the sun god and, as such, is the counterpart of Atum, the evening form of the sun god (see also *Scarab*).

Khnum Has the form of a ram. One of the most prominent creators, he forms material things and living creatures on his pottery wheel. In his work of creation he is assisted by Khnum gods, who he has also created. He was a local principal god in, among other places, Elephantine and Esna.

Khonsu He was, among others, moon god, who like Thoth subdivides time. At Edfu he had his own chapel (J), in which a leg was kept as his symbol.

Kiosk on Temple Roof A small temple with an approximately square ground plan, consisting of columns with architraves and screen walls between the columns, but without any fixed roof. The statues of the gods were carried up here during the New Year Festival in order to expose them—after having been concealed for so long in the interior of the temple—to the rays of the sun. The rays of the sun rejuvenated the statues and gave them new life force for another year. There is nothing left of the roof kiosk at Edfu except for the traces of its walls in the temple roof. The kiosk of Dendera has escaped destruction and is still standing on its site in the southwest corner of the roof.

Kites Isis and Nephthys as mourners (for Osiris) also appear as two birds, identified as kites.

Lector Priest Egyptian *khery-heb*. A high-ranking priest, who performed his duties in both mortuary and temple cults. He read the texts of the ritual and was a leading figure in the performance of festivals.

Library A small room (E'), set into the façade of the pronaos. It was the repository of the papyrus rolls containing the most important texts used in the cult, pattern books, and collections of texts. It also functioned as a sort of 'quick reference library' for the lector-priests. The inscriptions in the room have preserved the titles of some of the books, e.g., the books of 'Conducting the Ritual,' 'Overthrowing Seth,' 'Temple Inventory,' and 'Instructions for Decorating a Wall.'

Lion The door bolts of the temple were decorated with images of lions, which were regarded also in pharaonic Egypt as a symbol of power. Door bolts of this sort have been discovered by archaeologists.

The Living Ba of Ra in the Midst of His Children Ra, who has absorbed the form and nature of his children. In one version, the children are Shu, Osiris, and Khepry; in another version, Shu, Geb, and Osiris.

Maat Goddess and personification of the untranslatable concept *Maat*. It can be described as the principle of the correct and good performance of all things. Our concepts of 'truth' and 'justice' are only partial components of *Maat*. Conceived of as a substance it forms the nourishment of the gods. Maat, the daughter of Ra, was also regarded as the leader of the sun-god, as his Uraeus-snake and his eye. As embodiment of the gullet she allows words as well as food to pass.

Mehit Lion-headed goddess of the town of This in the Abydos nome. Consort of Onuris and as aggressive as he was. Also regarded as the Eye of Ra as well as the Uraeus-snake.

Menet Lion-headed warrior goddess, also regarded as the Eye of Horus.

Mesen Name of several cult places of Horus, most of them situated in the Delta. The name means perhaps 'place of the harpooner.' Horus killed his archenemy Seth with a harpoon whenever he appeared in the form of hippopotamus. 'Mesen(et)' was also the name of the chapel directly behind the sanctuary (I) as well as the name of the temple and the city of Edfu.

Min Principal god in the towns of Coptos and Panopolis. Min was depicted mostly with erect penis, since he was especially responsible for fertility (of vegetation, animals, and humans). He was also the Lord of the Eastern Desert and its products (particularly precious stones), and he was famed for his strength.

Names See *Royal Titulary.*

Naos The main fabric of the temple directly behind the Pronaos. Also, a general designation for the shrine with the statue of the deity.

Nemset-jars Water jars whose contents are drawn from the primeval waters. These waters had protective, revivifying, and especially rejuvenating effects.

Nest (of Falcon) The papyrus thicket of Chemmis.

Nome One of the administrative (and also religious) districts of ancient Egypt.

Nut The sky goddess, sister of the earth god, Geb. She gives birth to the sun in the morning, carries it on her body throughout the day and swallows it in the evening. She forms the vault of the sky with her body by standing on her hands and feet.

Obelisks Two of these monolithic granite pillars with pyramid-shaped peak once stood in front of the pylon of the temple of

Edfu, where they 'pierced those clouds of heaven,' that is, they fought against the thunder clouds, which were regarded negatively at Edfu. The expression also describes the great height of the obelisks.

Ointment-workshop Room Z in the temple, the so-called laboratory. On the walls are the recipes for producing salve-oils and incense preparations. The Lord of the (Ointment-)workshop might be the god Shesemu or Horhekenu.

Onuris Principal god of This in the eighth Upper Egyptian nome. Powerful hunter and warrior, whose favorite weapons were the lance and the spear.

Osiris Principal god of Abydos and Busiris. Murdered and resurrected god, Lord of the Underworld and Chief Judge of the Judgment of the Dead. God of cyclical rebirth, who renewed himself monthly and annually as the moon, the Nile inundation, and vegetation.

Perfect Seat A name of the Treasury (B').

The Permanent Ones A group of gods of the temple, who perform various activities. Thus they fill the eye of the moon and nourish Egypt. They may be divine ancestors or primeval gods. Other gods can also be called the Permanent Ones, e.g., Horus, Hathor, and Harsomtus.

Philometor Title of Ptolemies VI, IX, and X: 'the Mother-loving (God).'

Philopator Title of Ptolemies IV, VII , XII, and XIV: the 'Father-loving (God).'

Primeval Hill Mythological place, the first island to emerge on the morning of creation from the primeval ocean.

Principal God The principal divine occupant of any temple, believed to possess every conceivable characteristic and ability, from that of being the creator of the world to that of being the god of personal piety. The deity was also able to receive a guest cult in other temples, frequently only in one or more aspects, for example as creator, warrior, or lord of writing. The latter, the possible separation and free use of some of its characteristics, moves the deities of the Greco-Roman period in the direction of becoming concepts.

Pronaos The outer hypostyle hall (C').

Ptah Principal god of Memphis and one of the most respected creators who, as an artisan, created everything that exists.

Punt Country to the southeast of Egypt, which has not yet been precisely located. Punt, from the Old Kingdom, was the goal of Egyptian expeditions, which brought back from there all sorts of exotic products, especially myrrh and incense. In the temple inscriptions of the Greco-Roman period Punt was also regarded as the country from which the sun-god traveled every morning to Egypt.

Pure Corridor The area between the enclosure wall and the naos (I'–F' and fig. 3).

Pure Magazine A building outside the Enclosure wall in which the offerings for use in the cult were divided, set aside, and consecrated.

Pylon The mighty, twin-towered entrance building, which is much higher than the temple (K' and fig. 1). In Edfu its total height is about 70 cubits.

Ra His nature manifests itself above all in the sun, in which one can recognize his supreme power and authority over all things of this world. Thus, he is the creator and maintainer of creation and, as supreme judge, the guide of his creatures. In the daily and annual cycles alternating periods of strength and weakness can be detected: he is the youthful sun, which develops its strength, and the ageing sun, who needs help, who declines in order to be reborn anew.

Ra-Harakhty Principal god of Heliopolis, whose name reflects the amalgamation of two gods, Ra and Harakhty. The latter is Horus the falcon, who travels across the sky as Ra between the two horizons *(akhty)*. At Edfu Ra-Harakhty is equated with Horus Behdety. Therefore, his name can be added to that of Horus Behdety as an epithet; it can also replace the name Horus Behdety.

Royal Priest The king was ideally the first priest in all the temples of Egypt. In the daily cult his role was taken over by the Royal Priest.

Royal Titulary A five-part titulary, consisting of the *Horus* name, the *Two Ladies* name, the *Golden Horus* name, the *Throne* name, and the *Birth* name, the latter two written in cartouches. Each of these names opens a sequence of statements about the king. The first four names are assumed by the king as he ascends the throne, the last one when he is born. The Horus name characterizes the king as earthly representative of the god Horus; the Two Ladies name establishes a connection with the two Crown goddesses, Nekhbet (Upper Egyptian crown) and Uto (Lower Egyptian crown). The reading and meaning of the third name is still not certain. The Throne name associates the king with the two parts of the kingdom, Upper and Lower Egypt, while the Birth name characterizes the King as the son of the sun-god Ra.

Scarab Beetle (scarabaeus sacer), the form assumed by the morning sun (see also *Khepry*). Symbol of becoming and arising. Scarab amulets were very popular.

Season The year was divided into three seasons: *akhet* (inundation), *peret* (coming forth of what had been sown), and *shemu* (heat/dryness). Ideally, when the calendar was aligned with the solar year, the three seasons fell respectively from mid-July to mid-November, from mid-November to mid-March, and from mid-March to mid-July.

Seat of the First Festival A designation of both the kiosk on the temple roof and the Wabet. It was the scene of decisive rituals in the New Year Festival.

Seat of the Talon A name of the sanctuary, used alongside the names 'Dwelling' and 'Throne Seat in the Temple Heaven.' 'Seat of the Talon' refers here to the processional bark named in the place (*Edfou* VII, 15, 4–6), in which Horus the Falcon of Edfu can put his talons when he comes out of the sanctuary in the bark (out of the temple, as out of the underworld up to heaven); 'Dwelling' refers to the portable shrine located in the same place, which circumscribes the private area of the god, when his statue (human form with falcon head) is carried along in it during the procession; the third name refers to the great shrine in the sanctuary, the permanent seat of the god. In other contexts, the 'Seat of the Talon' indicates more generally the place where someone or something (e.g., light) has taken up residence.

Sed Festival Festival in which the renewal of the king's vitality was celebrated, in theory after 30 years of rule had elapsed, but in practice mostly after shorter intervals. The wish 'millions of sed festivals' is to be understood in connection with the afterlife.

Sekhmet Lion-headed goddess, Eye of Ra, and Uraeus-snake. She had a dual nature: on the one hand, she was able to use her aggressive strength positively in order to protect; on the other hand, her aggression and anger always had to be pacified by means of rituals so that she would not use them against Egypt and its inhabitants.

Senut Festival A festival on day six of the (lunar) month, on which also the foundation ceremonies were performed for the building of the temple.

Seshat Goddess of writing, counting, and drawing.

Seth Murderer of his brother Osiris, in the Late Period (from about the middle of the first millennium B.C.) outlawed in many parts of Egypt. Although Seth on the one hand was detested, on the other hand certain characteristics of the god were highly esteemed, such as his strength and sexual potency. At Edfu, Seth is the absolute embodiment of evil; the texts only refer to him with invectives. The scenes of the Great Myth of Horus show Seth being harpooned by Horus, the former appearing in the shape of a crocodile or hippopotamus. Should Seth reveal himself in a thunderstorm, Horus combats him in the form of waterspouts on the roof of his temple.

Shu Son of the first god to exist, Atum, and thus the paragon of the good son who protects his father and is his father's legitimate successor. Personification of the breath of life and the god of the air who supports the sky.

Sothis Goddess of the Sothis star (the fixed star Sirius), which after a long period of invisibility reappears in the sky about mid-July. Because this date coincided with the inundation, Sothis was regarded as the one who announced the inundation and thus the goddess of the beginning of the year. Sothis was often equated with Isis.

Tatenen Personification of the primeval hill, closely associated with Ptah of Memphis as primeval and creator god.

Tefnut Daughter of Atum and sister of Shu. Eye of Ra and, in this capacity, often equated with Hathor, Sekhmet, and other goddesses. In her lioness form and as fire-spitting Uraeus-snake, she destroys the enemies of Ra.

This One A designation of Horus of Edfu, used particularly in connection with primeval time and the foundation of the temple.

Thoth The quintessential god of wisdom who possesses all conceivable knowledge. He is always present when justice, the law, and precision have to be administered in all areas of daily life as well as in the temple cult. His connection with Maat is particularly close. He usually appears in the form of an ibis or a baboon or as a human with an ibis head.

Tjaru Town on the north-east border of Egypt, in the ancient fourteenth nome of Lower Egypt, near modern al-Qantara. The home of Horus of Mesen, who was worshipped here as a lion. Between Tjaru and Edfu there was a close theological connection, so that Tjaru could be described as 'Lower Egyptian Edfu.'

Tomb In particular a place and means of rebirth, and in no way merely a place of eternal rest.

Two Lands A name of Egypt that recalls the fact that the unified kingdom of Egypt arose only after the merger of Upper (Nile Valley) and Lower (Delta) Egypt.

Uraeus-snake A rearing cobra worn on the forehead of kings and gods, spitting fire and clearing the way for its wearer by destroying his enemies. The Uraeus-snake is associated closely with the crowns and the eyes of the sun god (sun and moon) as well as with the goddess Maat.

Wabet A room in Greco-Roman temples (at Edfu room P), in which the divine statues were clothed and decorated with amulets, crowns, and insignia in preparation for their ascent to the temple roof and procession to the kiosk, where the decisive cult ceremony of the New Year Festival was performed, the union of the statues with the rays of the sun (see also *Seat of the First Festival*).

Well of Moistening The water from the well was used to clean the temple (likely by sprinkling). It was probably located in the eastern pylon tower or near its façade, outside the temple.

Wetjeset-Her '(Portable) Chair (Throne Seat) of Horus' or '(Place that) Elevates Horus'; apart from Behdet one of the most commonly used names for Edfu.

Winged Disk The sun which, with the help of a pair of wings, crosses the sky every day. As an organic combination of Ra (sun disk) and Horus (wings) the Winged Disk became an emblem of Horus of Edfu (see also *Apy*).

Chronological Table

(all dates B.C.)

380–342 (Thirtieth Dynasty)	Last indigenous Egyptian dynasty
342–332 (Thirty-first Dynasty)	Second Persian Occupation
332–305	Alexander the Great and the Macedonian Occupation
305/4–283/2	Ptolemy I Soter I
283/2–246	Ptolemy II Philadelphos
246–222	Ptolemy III Euergetes I
222–205/4	Ptolemy IV Philopator
205/4–180	Ptolemy V Epiphanes
180–164	Ptolemy VI Philometor
170–163	Ptolemy VIII Euergetes II
163–145	Ptolemy VI Philometor
145	Ptolemy VII Neos Philopator
145–116	Ptolemy VIII Euergetes II
116–107	Ptolemy IX Soter II
107–88	Ptolemy X Alexander I
88–80	Ptolemy IX Soter II
80	Ptolemy XI Alexander II
80–58	Ptolemy XII Neos Dionysos
58–55	Cleopatra VI and Berenice IV
55–51	Ptolemy XII Neos Dionysos
51–30	Cleopatra VII (together with Ptolemy XIII, Ptolemy XIV, and Ptolemy XV Caesarion)
51–47	Ptolemy XIII
47–44	Ptolemy XIV
44–30	Ptolemy XV Caesarion

Rebel kings who broke loose from the central government and ruled in Upper Egypt

206–200	Haronnophris
200–186	Ankhonnophris
131–130	Harsiese

Bibliography

The publication of the Edfu Temple

Cauville, S. and D. Devauchelle, *Le temple d'Edfou*, revised edition of vols. I and II, Cairo, 1984 and 1987.

———, *Le temple d'Edfou*, vol. XV, Cairo, 1985.

Chassinat, É., *Le temple d'Edfou*, vols. IV–XIV, Cairo, 1929–34.

Chassinat, É., *Le Mammisi d'Edfou*, Cairo, 1939.

Chassinat, É. and M. de Rochemonteix, *Le temple d'Edfou*, vols. II and III, Cairo, 1918 and 1928.

de Rochemonteix, M., *Le temple d'Edfou*, vol. I, Cairo, 1897.

Works cited and further reading

Alliot, M., "Le culte d'Horus à Edfou au temps des Ptolémées," *Bulletin d'Égypte* 20, Cairo, 1949/1954.

Belzoni, G.B., *Narrative of the Operations and Recent Discoveries in Egypt and Nubia*, London, 1820.

Borchardt, L., *Das Grabdenkmal des Königs S'a³hu-Re^c*, vol. I, Leipzig, 1910.

Brunner-Traut, E., *Ägypten: Kunst- und Reiseführer mit Landeskunde*, 5th edition, Stuttgart, 1986.

Cauville, S., "Essai sur la théologie du temple d'Horus à Edfou," *Bulletin d'Égypte* 102, 1987.

————, *Edfou*. Cairo: Institut Français d'Archéologie Orientale, 1984.

de Cenival, J.-L. and H. Stierlin, *Ägypten: Das Zeitalter der Pharaonen*, Munich, 1964.

de Wit, C., "Inscriptions dédicatoires du temple d'Edfou," *Chronique d'Égypte* 36, 1961, 56–97 and 277–320.

Denon, V., *Voyage dans la Basse et la Haute Égypte*, Paris, 1802.

Description de l'Égypte, Paris 1809 ff.

Devauchelle, D., "Les graffites démotiques du toit du temple d'Edfou," *Bulletin de l'Institut Français d'Archéologie Orientale* 83, 1983.

Edwards, A., *A Thousand Miles up the Nile*, London, 1877.

Effland, A., "'*Nunmehr ein offenes Buch . . .*': Eine weitere Etappe der 'Wiederentdeckung' des Tempels von Edfu," *Kemet* 7:4, 1998, 60ff.

Fairman, H.W., *The Triumph of Horus*, London, 1974.

Flaubert, Gustave, *Notes de voyages* in: *Oeuvres Complètes de G. Flaubert*, Louis Conard, ed., Paris, Librairie-Editeur, 1910.

Gardiner, A.H. and A.M. Calverley, *The Temple of King Sethos at Abydos*, vol. III, London and Chicago, 1938.

Granger, N., *Relation d'un voyage fait en Égypte en l'année 1730*, Paris, 1745.

Helck, W. and E. Otto, *Lexikon der Ägyptologie*, vol. I, Wiesbaden, 1975.

Jenkins, K. and H. Küthmann, *Münzen der Griechen*, Munich, 1972.

Kurth, D., "Die Dekoration der Säulen im Pronaos des Tempels von Edfu," *Göttinger Orientforschungen (GOF)*, IV:11, Wiesbaden, 1983.

————, *Treffpunkt der Götter: Inschriften aus dem Tempel des Horus von Edfu*, Zurich and Munich, 1994; 2nd edition, Düsseldorf and Zurich, 1998.

————, "The Present State of Research into Graeco-Roman Temples," S. Quirke, ed., *The Temple in Ancient Egypt*, London, 1997, 152–58.

————, *Die Inschriften des Tempels von Edfu*. Abteilung I: Überset-
zungen, vol. 1, "Edfou VIII," Wiesbaden, 1998.

————, *Die Inschriften des Tempels von Edfu*. Begleithefte: 1 (sev-
eral authors), "Edfu: Studien zu Ikonographie,
Textgestaltung, Schriftsystem, Grammatik und
Baugeschichte," 1990; 4 (several authors), "Edfu: Studien zu
Vokabular, Ikonographie und Grammatik," 1994; 5 (several
authors), "Edfu: Bericht über drei Surveys: Materialien und
Studien," 1999; 6 (forthcoming 2004).

————, *Die Inschriften des Tempels von Edfu*. Abteilung I: Überset-
zungen, vol. 2, "Edfou VII," Wiesbaden, forthcoming 2004.

Lane, E.W., *Description of Egypt*, J. Thompson, ed., Cairo, 2000.

Lange, K. and M. Hirmer, *Ägypten: Architektur, Plastik, Malerei in
drei Jahrtausenden*, 5th edition, Munich, 1975.

Megally, M., "Two Visitors' Graffiti from Abûsîr," *Chronique d'É-
gypte* 56, 1981.

Petrie, W.M.F., *The Royal Tombs of the Earliest Dynasties* II,
London, 1901.

Sauneron, S., ed., "Le Voyage en Égypte du Vénitien anonyme
(Août–Septembre 1589)," *Voyages en Égypte des années
1589, 1590 et 1591*, Cairo, 1971.

Sauneron, S. and H. Stierlin, *Die letzten Tempel Ägyptens: Edfu und
Philä*, Zurich and Freiburg, 1978.

Shaw, Ian and Paul Nicholson, *The British Museum Dictionary of
Ancient Egypt*. Cairo: The American University in Cairo Press,
1995.

Sicard, C., "Œuvres III, Parallèle Géographique de l'ancienne
Égypte et de l'Égypte moderne: Présentation et notes de S.
Sauneron et M. Martin," *Bulletin d'Égypte* 85, 1982.

Traunecker, C. and J.-C. Golvin, *Karnak: Resurrection d'un site*,
Fribourg, 1984.

Wildung, D., *Ägypten: Von der prähistorischen Zeit bis zu den
Römern*, Cologne, 1997.

Illustration Sources

Fig. 1: Chassinat, *Edfou* IX, pl. IV.

Fig. 2: Chassinat, *Edfou* VII, p. 7.

Fig. 3: Chassinat, *Edfou* IX, pl. IX.

Fig. 4: Map courtesy of OasisPhoto.com.

Fig. 5: Chassinat, *Edfou* XI, pl. CCLXIX.

Fig. 6: *Description de l'Égypte*, vol. I, pl. 18.

Fig. 7: Helck and Otto, *Lexikon*, vol. I, 400, fig. 1a and b (after A. Badawy).

Fig. 8: Petrie, *Royal Tombs* II, pl. XVI.

Fig. 9: Adapted from Brunner-Traut, *Ägypten*, 483.

Fig. 11: de Cenival and Stierlin, *Ägypten*, 10.

Fig. 10: Photograph J.-P. Graeff, Hamburg.

Fig. 12: Adapted from Borchardt, *Grabdenkmal*, vol. I, pl. 5.

Fig. 13: Gardiner and Calverley, *Temple of King Sethos*, vol. III, pl. 37.

Fig. 14: Megally, "Visitors' Graffiti," 228.

Fig. 15: J.-P. Graeff, Hamburg.

Fig. 16: K. Croll, Düsseldorf.

Fig. 17: © University College London, Institute of Archaeology.

Fig. 18: Kurth, *Edfu* Begleitheft 6.

Fig. 19: Devauchelle, "Les graffites démotiques," pl. XV.

Fig. 20: Denon, *Voyage*, pl. 57.

Fig. 21: *Description de l'Égypte*, vol. I, pl. 48.

Fig. 22: Chassinat, *Edfou* XIV, pl. DLXXXVII.

Fig. 23: Photograph by the author.

Fig. 24: Photograph by the author.

Fig. 25–27: Jenkins and Küthmann, *Münzen*, nos. 566, 569, 570.

Fig. 28–31: URL: *www.wildwinds.com*, summer 2003.

Fig. 32: Chassinat, *Edfou* IX, pl. XXIVb.

Fig. 33: Chassinat, *Edfou* IX, pl. XXIb.

Fig. 34: Chassinat, *Edfou* IX, pl. XII.

Fig. 35: Chassinat, *Edfou* IX, pl. XI.

Fig. 36: Chassinat, *Edfou* IX, pl. XXXIIa.

Fig. 37: Chassinat, *Edfou* IX, pl. XXXIVb.

Fig. 38: Chassinat, *Edfou* IX, pl. XXXIIIc.

The ground plan and section of the temple on the inside covers are adapted from Sauneron and Stierlin, *Die letzten Tempel*, 36f.